WHAT ARE

What are Saints?

Fifteen Chapters in Sanctity

C. C. Martindale

Sheed and Ward
London

CONTENTS

CONTENTS

FOREWORD

THESE 'talks' were broadcast from London, Birmingham, Nottingham (thanks to special arrangements very courteously made by the Albert Hall there), and Manchester, on fifteen Sundays, from January 24th to May 8th, 1932. A very great number of letters was received from members of various denominations or of none, asking that they should be printed, and often the words 'verbatim,' or, 'without any change' were added.

The liberality of the B.B.C. permits me indeed to print them; and I have kept as close as seemed reasonably possible to what was actually said. The introductory talk was not, however, spoken as it is printed. I had not realised, till the last moment, that the introduction and the talk on St. Paul were to be given on the same Sunday. I had therefore very much to abbreviate the introduction. It is printed here, accordingly, at a somewhat greater length than it had when spoken.

Moreover, I had to keep, in those talks, as exactly as possible to fifteen minutes. Hence it was, throughout, an affair of compression. In the following pages I expand, very slightly, what I said, but chiefly, by quoting rather more (when possible) of the actual words used by the Saint being spoken of; for, very special requests came in that, when manageable, some such words should be recorded. The personality of the Saint would 'live' the better for it. But in saying this, I am on the whole safeguarding the B.B.C.; for, if these pages profess to be records of what was said by means of it, it becomes in a sort of way responsible for them. I wish, then, to affirm that while I do not think I have anywhere substantially altered my broadcast words, the B.B.C. must not be regarded as having sponsored literally each printed word.

It would moreover, be an affectation to pretend that the B.B.C. was not rebuked for allowing so much as one of the following words to be broadcast. I do not propose to enlarge upon the controversy, especially as the 'other-than-R.C.' approbation of the idea of the 'talks' (and, I like to recall, of the talks themselves) so enormously surpassed in volume that of the rebukes as to render these, in reality, negligible. Not that one would neglect any sincere or courteous expression of opinion. But I beg to emphasise that the B.B.C. was rigidly fair. It had thought of a series of talks on 'Mysticism,' or on 'What is a Mystic?' This might have been too vague. But *'holiness'* has existed in this world. No complete knowledge of human nature is possible if one leaves it out of account. But what *is* it? 'What *is* a Saint?' To this, various answers, obviously, may be given. It would indeed have been odd if Catholics, who alone still 'canonise' men and women and prefix the official title 'Saint' to their names, should have been forbidden to say anything upon the subject. No one suggested that Anglicans should not be allowed to speak, if they wished to, about Laud; Quakers, about Penn; and indeed, on one Sunday my own talk was followed by an enthusiastic one about Livingstone. By all means. Be sure that the B.B.C. has received no protest from Catholics against *that!* Nor are these 'talks' to be accused of 'medieval obscurantism.' Neither St. Paul nor Don Bosco were, so far as I know, medievals. Nor were the 'talks' to be regarded as muzzle-worthy because they would suggest certain 'values' in which not every Englishman believes. What talk about Mussolini, Napoleon, Luther, Barbarossa, but would express some estimate as to values in which not everyone would concur, unless the talks were so 'neutral-minded' as to be absolute wash-outs—I use the slang phrase deliberately! Nor was the B.B.C. to be deterred by the suggestion that no doubt I would be 'skilful' and not allow my insidious propaganda to be perceived. The poor R.C.! If he offends people, well—he has been 'offensive,' and that mustn't be tolerated. But if he doesn't, ah! the skilful creature! Traditional Jesuitry! Still, people were right in assuming that I would not be talking just about 'unusual ladies or gentlemen,' to quote the phrase, enshrined within one 'protest,' that gave such joy to most of those who read it.

Better accept it thus—if the B.B.C. proposed to allow certain great Christians to be spoken of, either it had to assume that no Catholic had ever been a Christian, or greatly Christian—and that would have been too nonsensical for anyone's ears—or it had to say that although some Catholics had been greatly Christian, no Catholic should mention them, and so engineer an antecedent probability of an imperfect understanding of the subject in hand reaching its listeners; just as it might fear would happen if it turned *me* on to a broadcast series of Wesleyan Worthies, of Jansenist or Theosophist notabilities, or silhouettes of Mrs. Eddy, Aimée Macpherson, John Knox, or Leo Taxil. Enough. I have tried to say *why* I think the persons I have chosen *were* great Christians, each in his separate and most personal way; and I observe that nowhere have I had to embark on 'controversy,' that is, on the task of showing that *someone else is wrong*. I derive no pleasure from doing that. I like to do homage to what is manifestly right—in these cases, splendidly and heroically right. Or, if indeed, I have to insist that certain principles of life are wrong—such as, that Money at all costs is what I must try to get; that Self-indulgence is as good as Self-control; that Self-control is enough without Self-sacrifice—well, I couldn't be a Christian at all without asserting *that*. In fact, I have had to balance, against letters saying: 'Thank you for showing what Catholics really believe in and prize,' others that contained two-edged compliments indeed, like: 'Your talks might have been given by an earnest *Presbyterian*. . . .' I don't think they could have; hardly anyone else thought that they could have; but I hope it wasn't just 'skilfulness' that made it possible for people to think that they could have. I would far rather trust that I spoke with my eye singly on my subject, and with my mind in charity with all men.

C. C. MARTINDALE, S.J., London, 1932

WHAT ARE SAINTS?

INTRODUCTORY

'WHAT is a Saint?' The answer to that, or part of it, ought to emerge from these talks, and not be offered at the outset. For if you start with a definition, you are apt to twist your evidence till it suits the definition.

One point, however, I would like to make at once. The word 'saint' has got rather under the weather. Words do deteriorate like that—as 'temperance' has done, till it practically means just abstinence from alcohol; or 'charity,' which has sunk to implying just the gift of coins; or 'liberal,' which suggests something to do with a political party. 'Saint' and 'saintly' are not words that are very popular nowadays. 'Sancti-monious' has definitely a bad significance, and at once suggests hypocrisy, or at least a sort of universal disapprobation of ordinary men and their behaviour. When introducing your friends, you do not usually say: 'Meet my friend Bill—a very saintly man . . .' You would be surprised if, when someone made a list of adjectives by which to describe a favourite film-star, a popular athlete, let alone an eminent financier or politician, the word 'saintly' were included. On the other hand, you *might* remark, with the kindliest twinkle in your eye: 'We'll take Jack along with us. He's a bit of a saint: but you'll like him'; and you would mean that, while being all that a good companion should be, he had set his ideals, his standards, rather higher than the average man might do and lived up to them, however quiet he might keep about it. And, in short, when a man says: 'Of course, I'm no *saint*, but I do draw the line somewhere . . .' he is in reality paying something of a compliment to Saints, because he implies that he is most anxious not to be thought a boaster, let alone a critic—he knows he falls pretty short of the first-rate—still, the first-rate does exist, and he pays homage to it just by confessing that he *is* not it.

13

The first thing, then, to say is this—Saints were *persons*. I am going to talk about real persons who lived; men so many feet and inches tall and weighing so many pounds; who said things; who looked into other people's eyes; and whom other people liked or else disliked. Saints are not theories, nor fictions. Of course there are plenty of Saints—men and women with 'St.' traditionally prefixed to their names—of whom history has very little to tell. Why, there are some whose very names are unknown, like most of those Forty Martyrs of Sebaste who were frozen to death upon an icy lake, within sight of a fine fire and hot drinks, rather than renounce Christ. They are rather like those countless soldiers buried in Flanders cemeteries, upon whose tombstones are engraved the words: 'Known to God.' (How have I done homage to the man, also unknown as far as I am concerned, who was inspired to provide that ample epitaph !) They are better even than our 'Unknown Soldier' who, though a real man once upon a time, has become a sort of collective symbol. No. The Saints I have chosen to speak of were real men, solidly established in history and who have *altered human life*.

They have altered it even to the insignificant degree of providing half of us with our Christian names. Certainly I regret it, when a country equips its children as often as not with names that have no Christian background. I would prefer to be called Cyril, rather than Cyrus; I would prefer a girl to be called Mary, rather than Ruby. It anyhow remains that Saints are not only Facts, but Forces. People by the million are to-day trying to manage their lives, even, to change their lives, to ennoble their lives, because of some man or woman, boy or girl, who long ago earned the title 'Saint.' I may admire Julius Cæsar or Cromwell or the philosopher Kant. But I do not, no, I do not love them as I love my living friends, and try to be like them, or to please them, or to deny myself as they did, because they did, and because I think they would like me to. Yet to-day how many thousands of our contemporaries are trying to mould their lives according as they think St. Francis, St. Teresa, St. Dominic, St. Ignatius—not only 'would have wished' them to, but (they believe) actually are wishing them to ! Saints were, and *are*, real and living persons, with whom millions of other living people hold they can get into vital contact, and certainly do manage their lives on that assumption. And, they consider, experience bears them out. The thing succeeds.

But what in the world has made a certain selection of people survive the ages thus—not merely as memories, but as un-dying actualities ?

Certainly not just Beauty. It might have been pleasant had all the Saints been very muscular, lissome, and good-looking people. Alas! plenty of them were ill; plenty of them, ugly. And no need to worry about this. The man is a fool who thinks personality has anything to do with physique, or that character is not seen in a face quite independently of its features.

And it would have been nice if all the Saints had been mighty thinkers or learned men of science; but they weren't. You don't need to know much about human nature before you realise that character, nay, that true understanding, lie much deeper than erudition does, or than subtle philosophies do. Indeed, you have almost given up expecting to find a lastingly interesting personality among those who describe themselves as the 'intelligentsia.' There can be a certain charm about the innocent student who knows all about Sanskrit but he can also be rather an ass.

And it would have been interesting if the Saints had all played prominent parts in politics or finance or society, and still more startling had politicians or financiers been usually Saints; but hitherto neither with politics, nor finance, nor social elegance have we associated as a rule either sanctity or the substantial betterment of mankind. If a Saint was also a man of affairs, like Pope Hildebrand or Sir Thomas More; or an artist, like St. Francis of Assisi, or a hard-headed man of the world like St. Ambrose or St. Aloysius, he was not a Saint because of it; but because, being all that, he infused into those qualities *something else*.

The first thing that was infused into his life was, Belief in God. Belief in GOD, not like the belief you have that it takes a certain number of light-years for the radiance of a star to reach you—a fact you cannot realise and that honesty doesn't matter to you in the slightest; but, like your belief in the invisible air without which you *know* you cannot breathe; belief in the love of a friend that no event, however inexplicable would be acknowledged by you as *disproving*, Cut God (were it possible) out of a Saint's life, and there would be nothing to which you could compare the appalling tragedy. Think of an artist who simply 'lived for' colour, and then went blind. Even he could *remember*, somewhat as Beethoven, grown deaf, could *think*, though never hear, his music. But Life, without God, would, for the Saint, simply *die out*. Again, the Saint lives for, and in God, not simply as the Mohammedan mystic (for example) might do so. He reaches God as God intends to be reached, through Christ, and in Christ. I know that people speak of Buddhist saints, Confucian saints, but this is (to be realist) a misnomer, because we are perfectly aware that normally we mean, by 'Saint,' at least a Christian. When St. Justin himself spoke of 'Christians before Christ,' he knew quite well he was using a bold paradox. I, anyway, shall be speaking about Christian Saints. Very well. Amazing as may be the identity of mind and feeling that can come about between two human friends, or between man and woman truly and thoroughly in love with one another and lastingly so, this is as nothing to the 'interpenetration' of the Saint's mind, and Christ's mind: the unification of the Saint's heart, with Christ's Heart: the indwelling in the Saint, of Christ's own Spirit.

Yet Christ, living in His Saint, will not *substitute Himself* for the personal life of that Saint. The Saint will retain his most marked personality; his personal characteristics will not be overlaid by, smudged out by, distorted by, his sanctity. Indeed, I have chosen to speak, on the whole, of Saints of most remarkable personality. Saints of different centuries, different nationalities, different social environments. Each, in his age, in his place, finds his 'self' enhanced and made more 'personal' by reason of that in-dwelling Christ who becomes at once the Soul within his soul, and his supreme driving power.

For, the third thing you will see about the Saints is, their tremendous influence on other men. Even a would-be 'hermit,' like St. Anthony, wielded and wields (little as we guess it) a colossal influence. They did not *argue:* 'Because God loves mankind, therefore I ought to do so too'; but, having in them 'that mind which also was Christ Jesu's,' having in them a heart like to His Heart, they forthrightly love; they love intensely; they serve to the ultimate limit of self-sacrifice and beyond it.

I think, then, that we can safely say, before so much as embarking upon the actual history of certain 'Saints,' that Saints are, anyway, real and historical persons, who survive, not just as memories, but as forces, and do so, because they had something *special* in them—were not just men of flamboyant vision like Cecil Rhodes, or of sweeping unscrupulous genius like Napoleon, nor just Quixotes, let alone folk of personal charm or beauty—mere modern Helens of Troy, an up-to-date Adonis. The speciality that was theirs can be shown to be, in all cases, an *intense* belief in God: an *intense* love for Jesus Christ; and *intense* devotion, for Their sakes, to the service of mankind (albeit in the most widely divergent *ways*—but still, always the service and salvation of their fellow-human for Christ's sake). I shall not altogether confine myself to men who have been *placarded* as Saints; who have had, as I said, the prefix 'St.' officially placed before their name. I hope to finish with a few who may, no doubt, win that honour in the future. But not only are there myriads of unknown, unnamed Saints, besides the official ones; but, thank God, Sanctity is not the affair of one century rather than another. Precisely because, when Sanctity is spoken of, *God* is being spoken of, and *Christ*, and *Souls*, therefore it is an enduring phenomenon and a glory in the human race, and as ageless as Christ is.

.   .   .   .   .

The short passages between the 'Saints' were not broadcast. It is hoped that a series upon women saints (who cannot possibly be omitted from any proper view of sanctity) may be broadcast, after a due interval.

Our Lord Jesus Christ surrounded Himself with certain men to whom He gave His special love and confidence. Among these were, for instance, St. Peter and St. John, of whom we would gladly have spoken, but they in their turn collected around themselves men whom they could trust, and who were animated by a like spirit with their own. Such, little by little, became, for example, St. Mark, who would well have deserved a 'talk.' But head and shoulders among the 'second generation,' so to call it, of Christians, stands out St. Paul. It is of him therefore that I begin by speaking.

*

ST. PAUL

D. PROBABLY A.D. 67.

JUST before the coast of Asia Minor swings south towards Palestine, is a small triangle of soil among huge mountains— Cilicia. In it, upon the Cydnus, stands the town Tarsus. For a thousand years before Christ, Greeks, Assyrians, Persians, Syrians, Jews, and, last of all, the Romans, had poured into the land ; Julius Cæsar himself had fascinated the town and for a while it re-named itself Juliopolis. When he was murdered, Anthony went there to visit his half-of-the-world, and Cleopatra, with purple sails and silver oars, was carried up the Cydnus to visit him. But the town had retained its proud personality and had deserved to do so. To maintain and develop itself, it had literally hurled its river this way and that, the stream that used to run now in driblets, and now torrential and yellow, making the plain a mere marsh horrible with malaria. It had established the shifting coastline with solid quays, huge docks and warehouses; inland, behind the steaming orchards, its merchants had built opulent villas on the foot-hills; and even through the Taurus range, that rock-wall over 4,000 feet high behind them, chisels had carved a carriage-road with cliffs sheer 600 feet this side and that, for trade to pass over the bleak uplands with their boulders, salt-crusted lakes, and heaths, and descend once more to the vast emporiums like Ephesus or Smyrna, and set forth, westward, to Greece, to Italy, Spain or Gaul, or Britain. High above even these aristocrats of trade, lived Roman Citizens of Tarsus, proud as princes.

In, then, this town, heiress of so many centuries, a boy was born when our Lord may have been but fifteen years of age. He was named Saul, after the first king of Israel, his family being

Jewish, of the tribe of Benjamin. His father, Roman citizen, yet intensely Jewish, sent his son, aged about 13 to Jerusalem to be educated by the famous Rabbi Gamaliel. The education was traditional, narrowly religious, fiercely nationalist.

Even though proud of his citizenship and able fully to appreciate the grandeur and the structure of the Roman Empire, Saul was to grow up passionately Jewish. He was to be above all, 'Hebrew, son of Hebrews; Pharisee, son of Pharisees: according to the strictest sect of our religion I lived a Pharisee'; he was 'irreproachable' even as to the ten thousand regulations with which tradition had overlaid the Law of Moses.

Back in Tarsus during our Lord's brief public life, he never actually met Him: but he was again in Jerusalem just when St. Stephen provoked his listeners to frenzy by proclaiming that the Jesus whom they had crucified was the Christ, their King; and while they were battering Stephen into pulp with stones the youth was grimly keeping guard over the cloaks they had thrown off. He was 'approving everything that was being done'; went straight to the high priest to get leave to exterminate the new sect; forced his way into private houses and dragged both men and women to prison; and, says he (when the memory of those days had become a haunting nightmare), 'in my excess of madness I would pursue them even into distant cities.' They fled, in fact to Damascus, and thither, 'breathing out threats and murder,' he followed.

The city was already gleaming white amid its orange-groves, when a light shone for him that outdazzled the noon, and from the light, a vision, and a voice. 'Saul, Saul, why persecutest thou me?' 'Who art thou?' 'I am Jesus, whom thou art persecuting.' 'Lord, what wouldst Thou have me do?' 'Stand up, enter the city, and it shall be told thee what thou must do . . .' Blind, led by the hand, he stumbled into Damascus, was received by the frightened Ananias, and was baptised.

See then here a whole life violently uprooted; a mind turned upside down; a career of flaming publicity, of nationalist ferocity, extinguished; a prospect of meeting with but rage on the part of his one-time allies, and with, at best, a chill bewilderment on the part of Christians still bleeding from the wounds that this terrifying convert had inflicted on them. No wonder he plunged into the hidden deserts of Arabia to recapture his very wits; to steel his will for the future struggle; to pray his way into the very heart of the mystery that had been revealed to him—that *Christ was one with His Christians*—'Why persecutest thou *Me ?*'—that *Christ was within himself*—'Christ was revealed *in me*'—and to assimilate the enormous charge that had been laid on him—that he was to be *world*-Apostle. 'Thou art like a casket specially chosen, within which My Name is to be carried far—even to the pagans.'

Clearly I cannot, in these few minutes, even outline to you this man's further life: his return to Palestine and gradual acceptance by the apostles; his clashes with the Jews as the arch-apostate; his active life, beginning round Tarsus itself; then gradually taking in all Asia Minor; its Romanised towns; its ancient stony villages in the unsophisticated uplands that he liked so much; down then into its feverish coast-cities, commercial yet fanatically religious centres like Ephesus, a sort of Shanghai crossed with Mecca; then over into Europe, planting himself, for example, at Philippi, a nerve-centre of the military and trade-life of the Empire, and at Thessalonika, that half of you remember as Salonika. Nor his descent into delicate, cultured Athens, where they politely laughed at him; and into Corinth, city of trade and blatant immorality, which welcomed him far better. Nor of his journey to Rome (his shipwreck off Malta is described with glorious vivacity by St. Luke, his doctor and chronicler); nor can I explain why I think it certain he went afterwards to Spain and conceivably even into Britain.

I can't even properly describe his character—his genius or friendship, his quivering sensitiveness, his exquisitely responsible gratitude, his passionate *interest* in everything—why, in athletics ! He says he has his race to run, and *runs* it, in no doubt about his goal; he fights, not like a man who is *shadow-boxing*—his almost motherly tenderness, his white-hot earnestness of conviction; his attention to smallest details, the sublimity of his ideal; his total disregard of physical pain, of dangers from brigand or from secret assassin, or from official police, or from sea or from fire. I can't even express to you his delightful sense of humour; his perfect courtesy; the obstinate courage required for his monotonous work, first trying (and failing) to persuade his fellow-Jews, and then trying to convince the pagan populations (and succeeding), and again, straining to keep his converts loyal to the Faith they had professed. And all this, being a man small, ugly, constantly ill, often feeling horribly frightened, desperately lonely. I say this, not out of my head, but able to prove each word from his own letters.

I will then, single out two points only. One a thing that he did; the other, why he did it.

Across the enormous square surrounding the midmost of the Temple of God in Jerusalem stood a wall; on a marble tablet was engraved the statement that it was death for any non-Jew to penetrate beyond it. Christ, said Paul, has '*broken down* the dividing wall'; God's Fatherhood, Christ's brotherhood, and Saviourhood, are for all men, pagans no less than Jews. That, from the outset, had been the Christian doctrine: the other Apostles had proclaimed it and acted on it. But Paul declared that his personal *vocation* was to preach that truth among the pagans specially. 'Nay,' he cried out, 'there *exists* now no more Jew versus Greek, no more free man versus slave—nay, no more male versus female—you are all One Person in Jesus Christ.' 'To be circumcised, to be uncircumcised—that is nothing—but, a New Creation !'

And he preaches this (as I said all Saints live their life) *intensely*. 'Of this Gospel was I made minister by the free gift of Grace given me according to the energising of His power. His power that is *on the scale of the Energy of the Might of His Strength* that He made to act in the person of Christ. Ah, to me, the least of all Christians, was given this grace—to announce to the *pagans* the unfathomable riches of Christ' . . . yes, 'for *this* I strain and struggle in the measure of that Energy of His that energises so mightily in ME.'

Strange thought, that but for the energy of this man, itself derived from the power of God in Christ, there would not be

this day that great dark dome of St. Paul's that overlooms the
Thames. But may St. Paul bequeath to you much more than
any dome—domes, after all, some day are bound to fall. What,
then, must he supremely give to you ?

The source of all that creed, that vitality; simply, Christ.
What did he feel about himself? That he was 'Bruised, but
not broken; dismayed, yet not despairing; hunted, yet not
fainting; stoned, but never slain—ever bearing about in our
very body the killing of the Lord Jesus, so that the *Life* of
Jesus may be revealed in this our dying flesh ! . . . *Therefore*
play we not the coward; but even though our outward man be
being worn away, yet from day to day is our inner self made
new; for the trivial anguish of the moment works out for us
overwhelmingly, overwhelmingly an eternal weight of glory,
for we look—not on things visible, but on things unseen.
What we see, endures but for an hour—the Unseen is eternal !'
'Oh, I reckon the sufferings of the present moment as not
worthy to be counted in view of the glory destined to be
revealed in our regard. If GOD is for us, who can be against us?
Who is going to lay charge against God's Chosen ? *God* . . .
But God makes us *just!* Who shall condemn us ? Christ ?
But He died—rather, He rose, He is at God's side, interceding
for us. Ah—who shall separate us from that love of Christ ?
Shall affliction, or persecution, or hunger, or nakedness, or
dangers, or the sword; (all that can and does separate us
poor humans from one another) ?. . . But in these *very*
things we more than conquer, through Him who loved us. Ah,
I know well, that neither life nor death, nor angels nor spirits,
nor the present nor the future, nor height nor depth nor anything created shall be able to separate us from the Love of God
that is in Christ Jesus our Lord.'

No wonder, then, that at long last the aged Apostle, left
alone in his underground prison at Rome, could look back in
perfect peace on all of his life—the packed uproarious cities
and the moorland villages, the seas and the foreign lands,
right back to his babyhood at Tarsus, with its walled-in
waters and hot orchards—yes, and from amid the thronging
memories of friends, he needed not to exclude the face of

Stephen shining like an angel's through the blood, nor of all those Christian men and women he had sent freezing into death. Now his own time had come.

The half-dozen soldiers hurried him out, down through squalid slums to the Tiber, with his back to the theatres and palaces and temples and all of the golden, rosy Rome of Nero, and then, by the Ostian road, three miles, till they turned off to the left, into a little pinewood where medicinal springs flowed. Old, sick, lonely, very tired, Christ's servant was stripped, for the last time flogged, tied to a pine-tree, and beheaded. (You can still kneel there, for the site is ascertained. The place is silent, save for the eucalyptus leaves that whisper above the murmuring waters, and for the voice of prayers.) Friends were allowed to remove the body to a spot somewhat nearer Rome, and in time a different Emperor placed above the tomb the inscription that still is ours—PAUL, APOSTLE, MARTYR. He who had proved that during his earthly years life *was* for him just 'Christ'—'I live—no more just *I*—but Christ is living in me'— now lives, according to his favourite phrase of all, '*in Christ*,' still praying and still energising until such time as, throughout creation, Christ shall be 'All in all.'

A longer account can be found in the writer's *St. Paul*, in the series, "The Household of God" (Burns, Oates and Washbourne).

After the dispersal and death of the apostles, when even St. John, in his extreme old age, had died, a new generation of Christians took on the duty of defending the Christian Faith by their writing, adorning it by their lives, glorifying it by their death. You pass into the world of 'apologists' and of 'martyrs' —sometimes, as in the case of St. Justin (died A.D. 167), being both conscientious writers and pleaders on behalf of their creed, and being killed for it. The root of these persecutions was always the exorbitant imperial power—that Roman Empire which declared that there was nothing above it in regard of human life, and that its Emperor must be worshipped. You will see this worship of Human Power coming again and again into conflict with the Christian Conscience, that knows well that what is Cæsar's must indeed be given to him; but that what is God's must be reserved for God alone. Great bishops, like Polycarp and Ignatius from the East, died gladly as martyrs; men of high intelligence, like Irenaeus in Gaul, or the Africans, Tertullian and Cyprian, and in Egypt, Clement and Origen, applied their minds, with greater or less success, to the intellectual defence of Christianity. It was just after their period that St. Anthony was born.

*

ST. ANTHONY OF EGYPT

WHEN speaking of St. Paul, I suggested that part of his work consisted in keeping his converts loyal. The Church of Christ never was, and never professed to be, a sort of pious clique. Our Lord Himself pictured it as a field containing weeds as well as wheat; a net, having in it fish both pure and poisonous. The Church does not exist for men who are already good; but to help men to become good: her Sacraments are not prizes for the perfect, but much rather, medicines and tonics for the spiritually sick or weakly. Yet the Church is not a mere hospital for the morally diseased, or for religious casualties, or spiritual convalescents. The generous heart, the strong worker, the vivid imagination, the triumphant will—all these are catered for by her and called to live within her. Still, Christians are a mixed lot, and most men themselves are mixtures, as our own conscience tells us all too clearly; and I like to think, on the whole, of the Church as consisting of men who are *trying*, probably failing quite often, getting mauled and floored, but getting up again—and indeed, what can't happen in the ring, getting *helped* up again. We shall present ourselves to our Judge with plenty of black eyes and rainbow-coloured bruises administered by World, by Flesh, or by Devil momentarily successful; but He won't mind that: He will say: 'Well—anyway—you've *won!*'

I say all this because after two hundred and fifty years of Christianity, the level of the early enthusiasm, the standard of holiness, had sunk a good deal. No wonder. By that time, Christianity was becoming popular; and the net began to envelop people wholesale, and so contained a higher percentage of queer fish than it had done. Also, important persons of all sorts—politicians, officials, courtiers—were becoming Christians, and it is none too easy to find an *undiluted* character among these, or a behaviour that can always rhyme with conviction. They think they have to compromise, to be reticent, to consider the careers of their relatives, and so forth. And meanwhile, in enormous cities like Egyptian Alexandria, worldliness and vice among the pagan generality rose to a pitch that there was no public opinion about it at all, and the worst parts of, say, Port Said are respectable compared to what the effrontery of a large Egyptian city was then.

However, persecution could still occur. It broke out, under the emperor Decius. Christians fled to the deserts, and after a while stayed there by preference. The vile life of those cities stank in their memories. The towns had been too hateful, or too seductive. Just then, Anthony was born. He was well-to-do, and at eighteen inherited his parents' three hundred acres of rich Egyptian soil, and their fortune. But Christ's words: 'Go, sell what thou hast, and give it to the poor,' struck home to him. He handed over his land to the poor of his village; got rid of his capital; and went to seek, in the desert communities of Christians, for some experienced old man who should control his wayward, impressionable temperament which, he knew, he could not govern all alone. For fifteen years he lived a life of study in the great Egyptian solitudes till he found even these insufficient, and retired further to a dismantled fort on the Nile, where he lived on a load of bread brought to him every six months, and dates off the local palms. His friends visited him periodically, and found him always well.

You might suggest that this was a running away. Why didn't he stop in the towns, help his fellow-Christians, and, as they say, 'do good,' or anyhow something practical? Mooning among tombs! Shunting the rough-and-tumble of life off on to those who had pluck to cope with it! Well, I return to that in a moment. I will just say that anything destined to be strong and efficacious in *action* needs a drastic preparation of *character*. When Anthony knew himself, and could *govern* his most vigorous self, 'keep himself' thoroughly 'in order,' as they say, he would do all that exterior work too. Hasty self-production, self-advertisement, talk, rushing around—this never gets a man far, and the results don't last. And meanwhile, his reputation for shrewd spirituality and true knowledge of the world grew so fast that men simply flocked to him and made a colony around him; and, when persecution broke out afresh, he *did* leave his solitude and visit his suffering fellow-Christians at Alexandria and in the Sudan mines where they were imprisoned; such was the awe in which people already stood of his overwhelming personality, that he was never himself arrested, and could disregard the persecuting police with a nerve that never deserted him. After five or six years he went back, even deeper into solitude, across the Nile to a cliff that fronted the Red Sea. It says something for the *permanence* of his work that both his earlier monastery and this second one are still, after more than one thousand years and six centuries, existing and inhabited.

Here, then, he settled, cultivating enough ground around his cell to support himself. Below him, in the plains, thousands of monks had established themselves, and he went regularly down to visit, examine and advise them. Troops of people journeyed long distances to seek similar advice and had a hostel of their own; but, if they stayed any time, they had to work, on week-days, like the monks, at baking, weaving, and so on.

Here is, condensed, an anecdote that will show you the fashion of men's thoughts, in those days; and also, Anthony's method of dealing with people.

Elogios, 'struck by a passion for eternal things,' deserted the world's hubbub. But he grew lonely; met a cripple, and promised God that he would look after him till he died. The cripple, after fifteen years, fell sick. Elogios bathed, fed and cured him. With convalescence, came temper. The cripple raved at his benefactor, crying: 'Put me in the market-place. I want meat!' Elogios gave him meat. 'No—I want the crowds! Put me back where you found me!' Elogios was puzzled. 'Am I to cast him forth? But God and I have entered into compact. Am I to keep him? But to me he gives

bad days and nights. . . .' His friends said: 'Both of you go
to Anthony.' So they went. Now when people called on
Anthony he had them announced as from 'Jerusalem' or from
'Egypt,' according as their quest was sincere or frivolous.
'Which are these?' he asked. 'A mixture,' said his secretary.
Elogios entered first. Anthony said gravely: 'Thou wouldst
cast this man forth? But He who made him does not
cast him out. Thou wouldst cast him forth? But God raised
up the Fairer One than thou art, to gather him. . . .' Then
to the other, he said: 'Crooked and crippled soul! cease
thy fight with God! Knewest thou not that it was *Christ*
who served thee? For *Christ's* sake it was that Elogios made
himself thy servant.' He bade them farewell affectionately;
they went home friends, and died within three days of one
another.

Besides this, Anthony's influence began to exert itself like
a radiating force in other countries too—thus St. Hilarion
visited him about 310, and inaugurated monasteries in Palestine; Mar Agwin did so in 325 in Mesopotamia; St. Pachomius, nearer home, in 318. Anthony had two qualities proper
to great men—he was able (such was the force of his personality)
to leave almost complete freedom and initiative to the men
under his immediate influence: and he did not grumble if
others imitated but also modified his system—thus Pachomius
started a much more centralised, highly organised monasticism, with carefully planned departments concerned with
every sort of handicraft—gardening, carpentry, iron-work,
tanning, dyeing, cobbling, writing—a whole hive of useful
industry *not* carried on for gain.

It was this sort of monasticism that was destined to spread
in the West. Not only did the Christian Emperors come to
value the civilising as well as the spiritual genius of Anthony,
and what *they* said naturally travelled far, but that intellectual
giant, Athanasius of Alexandria, who knew and loved St.
Anthony, wrote his *Life*, and that travelled farther still, and
influenced, at a crisis, the life of St. Augustine himself, of whom
I hope to speak next time, and Augustine has influenced every
century in this our West until our own. And away in Southern

Italy, further off still in Gaul, further still in Ireland, types of monastic life were set up in direct descent from Anthony's. Nay, St. Benedict, 480–543, utilised, while he adapted, the kind of life taught by the Egyptian Saint, and thereby, I say deliberately, created one of the three forces that made Europe so much as possible. Why do I say that? Because when the Barbarians, the Huns, Goths, Franks, Vandals, swept into the western half of the Empire, they crashed up against three immovable facts—the Papacy, the Bishops with their cathedral churches and their schools, and the monasteries. A chaotic mind is always awe-struck by an orderly one; violence is impotent before fearlessness; moral or social anarchy very soon yield to a Will firmly set towards what is right, a way of life that tends steadily towards men's betterment. And the monasteries were centres of grim study, steadfast instruction, development of agriculture, of ever-improving handicraft, of respect for authority, of orderliness of mind, of discipline of the will. You never can begin to calculate what Europe, and England herself, owe to the monks. When Henry VIII, in desperate need of money, destroyed the monasteries, and handed over their lands and revenues to his favourites, he did what by itself would have sufficed to create the problem of poverty and unemployment even had there been no Industrial Revolution. Yet did he *not* destroy, even in this land, monasticism; not only would the best in our public school system, I think, have been impossible without the Benedictine tradition; there are more monks, we are told, now in England than before the religious revolution; the great educational houses—Ampleforth, Douay, Downside, and smaller ones, Ramsgate, Ealing, Belmont in Herefordshire; that positive magnet for visitors, Buckfast Abbey in Devon—built wholly by the hands of monks—are governed by Benedictine monks, sons of St. Benedict, who was the heir of Anthony.

Anthony died in 356, aged a hundred and five years, his sight and hearing unimpaired, and all his teeth sound in his head. His was a personality sublime, yet sane: commanding, colossal yet simple, shrewd, drily humorous, and affectionate, even tender; able to converse with politicians and philosophers, judges and generals, yet to make friends with the average man of market-place and shop. His will-power was tremendous, yet *controlled*, and never bursting forth into mere tyranny; his intelligence, accurate; his vision, sublime; yet never wild, never fanatical. This *hermit* was the most 'sociable,' most 'clubbable,' of men. What, then, is self-advertisement ? He used none of it, and yet seems as familiar to me as any aged man that I honour has been. And what is money ? He got rid of his, yet built a memorial as lasting as the pyramids, more meaningful than they. For who is grateful to, who does homage to, the builders of those colossal excrescences of stone ? What is position, social or political ? He sought neither—and which of the politicians or even emperors of his day, let alone the financiers, means anything to *us*—is *doing* anything now ? But Anthony is *active*.

And when I have been sailing through the Red Sea, and have watched the sun rise upon the westward mountains, and seen them change from grey to lavender, from lilac into daffodil and crocus, into rose-red and carnation, when have I not thought of the dawn of St. Anthony upon our world, and the warmth and splendour and vitality that he has left upon it and within it ? Why, it is really because of him, and by no means because of Anthony—friend, then foe, of Cæsar, and Cleopatra's lover—that any of you, named Anthony, is so called !

See Dom Cuthbert Butler: *The Lausiac History of Palladius;* and the writer's: *Upon God's Holy Hill, St. Anthony.*

I mentioned that St. Athanasius (d. 373) wrote the life of St. Anthony, and that the book played a decisive part in the conversion of St. Augustine, of whom I speak next. Other very great names might be mentioned—St. Cyril of Jerusalem (d. 386); St. Cyril of Alexandria (d. 444). Enough to say that this period of Christian history was one of intensive study, of brilliant intelligence—and needed to be, for, if the knowledge of the older world was to be developed and handed on at all, men of supreme mental energy had to achieve this; for the western world was about to be smashed into pieces by barbarian invasions, and the eastern was to become soon enough intellectually inert. Three names now stand out—the great ecclesiastical governor, St. Ambrose, Archbishop of Milan (d. 397); St. Jerome, that fierce old scholar, whose Latin translation of the Scriptures did more, maybe, to form the language of Europe for centuries than anything else did or could have done (d. 420); and St. Augustine himself (d. 430, aged seventy-six).

*

ST. AUGUSTINE

354–430

No one really knows how the modern world came into existence if he knows nothing about the man I am now to talk of. He lived at a moment when the Civilisation that held the world together was crashing even more completely than ours is. He was a man of *his* world, but also, the man of the world that preceded him and of the world that followed him. Had there been no Augustine, heaven knows in what barbarism we might now be wallowing.

He was born in North Africa, at Tagaste, November 13th, 354. His mother was Christian; his father pagan. The boy grew up, unbaptised, with a misty idea of God as a Great Someone, a hazy notion that there was a life hereafter, and a vague reverence for the name of Jesus. But he remained without any religion in particular, very keen on his games, hating *pain*, and enchanted by the beauties of Latin literature. Kind friends financed him so that he should go to the University of Carthage. And there he ran wild. He belonged to a gang—the *Eversores*—'Upset the lot of 'em'— and please be sure that in an African city of that century, a gang like that did not mean merely a pack of rowdy lads who go singing down the streets and smashing lamps. He regarded himself as 'absurd if innocent; preposterous, if pure —the greatest shame of all was, to feel ashamed.' In that extraordinary city of science, yet of favourite jockeys; of ecstatic pagan worship and of dance-girls; of captured gorillas exhibited as savage women, and sea-monsters shown as mermaids, he revelled in his wrong-doings till he fell in love with a girl to whom he remained for fifteen years the faithful slave. (I am not at all scorning her, no, nor him. Fidelity is much,

33

and not least in these our days of quickly won, quickly chucked.)
All the same, he was getting sick of his chaotic life. His very
love bred in him jealousy, suspicion, panic. He began to loathe
it. Even then, this tormented lad was praying: 'Give me
chastity—but not yet . . .' His mother, Monica, was
praying for him—one of the most exquisite characters that
history hands down to us. 'The son of so many tears,' a wise
old bishop said to her, 'never can be lost.'

A book that I shall mention when speaking next Sunday,
Cicero's *Hortensius*—a pagan book about virtue and vice
—made Augustine see that there was a *steady something* in the
line of *character* that could make his tempestuous passions
seem but trash. And first, despairing of full self-control, he
joined the 'Manichean' sect, which taught that *matter*, the
body, though essential to your *man*hood, was bad in itself.
Horrible insult to the Creator, who declared that all that He
had made was 'very good !' But meanwhile, it enabled him
to say that it was not *he*, really, who sinned, but just his body.
. . . Then he found that one's *will* counts for more than he
had thought. He spoke a brilliant speech against the blood-
thirsty iniquities of the Circus—and, behold, his friend
Alypius gave up going to those murderous shows on the
strength of it. . . . But *he* could not stay away. He bolted
from Africa and its vulgar horseplay, to Rome, hoping for
some seriousness, and opened a school of 'eloquence' there.
But he could not get his fees, and finally won a job at Milan.
But even there the emptiness of his life—teaching people to
make speeches, just imagine !—sickened him. He relapsed into
agnosticism. He felt it was just wiser to *doubt everything*. Out
of this hopeless state—for, where can you get, what can you
do, if everything is with equal probability true and false, right
and wrong ?—two things rescued him: the mystical doctrines
of the descendants of the Greek philosopher Plato, and the
overwhelming personality of St. Ambrose, Bishop of Milan.
Between the two he began to feel that he must be Christian,
or 'something else.' But *what* else ? There was no answer.
His two wills, 'one old,' he wrote, 'one new, one of the spirit,
one of the flesh, fought angrily together, and my soul was on

the rack.' Someone read the Life of St. Anthony to him; and:
'Thou, Lord, in his words wast twisting me back to myself
. . . wast setting me before my own face, that I might see
how foul I was, how distorted and filthy, how soiled and
ulcered. And if I tried to turn my gaze from myself, the
reader went on reading, and thou didst thrust myself once
more before my own eyes . . . till I lay naked to myself
. . . and I kept saying: Let it be now! Let it be now!
And as I spoke, I made towards the resolve, and I was all but
doing it, and I did it not. . . . Yet I stepped not wholly
back, but I would stand still hard by, and draw breath. And
again I would try . . . and all but—all but, I reached and
I held; and lo, I was not there, and I reached not, and held
not, fearing to die to death. . . . Those vanities, my loves of
yore, kept plucking softly at my robe of flesh, and softly
whispering—Wilt thou dismiss us? and from this moment
shall not this and that be allowed to thee any more for ever?'
But on the other side there seemed to stand the army of the
chaste, the strong: 'What these could do, cannot you?'
The words came back and back. And, one day, when he sat
desperate in his garden, a child's voice reached him singing
some nursery-rhyme—Take it, read it; take it, read it! And,
unrolling his Scriptures, he happened on the words: 'Not in
riotings and drunkenness and impurities, but put on the Lord
Jesus Christ, and make no provision for the flesh and its
lusts.' Suddenly, but calmly, the miracle was worked: Augustine was another man, and in 387 was baptised. Monica was
with him.

After a while he was ordained priest and became Bishop
of Hippo in North Africa, near Carthage. There, two years
ago, his fifteenth centenary was magnificently celebrated by
men from, literally, all parts of the world, and almost as
notably by Mohammedans as by Christians. Unable to go
myself, as I was ill, I felt compensated when I spoke in a church
dedicated to his honour, in the extreme south of Africa, a year
later. He died on August 28th, 430, his eyes fixed on a huge copy
of the Penitential Psalms that he had had fixed up before him.
His world was crumbling to pieces—Hippo was actually

being besieged by the Vandals; it was taken just after his death. I speak seriously when I assert that but for his influence that world might have stayed fallen. Certainly a world quite different from ours would, if any, have risen on the ruins. How was that?

I remind you that the West—Rome and the western empire —was growing ever more remote from the East—i.e. Constantinople. Riches, science, social glory, political power, seemed concentrating themselves over there. And hitherto practically all intellectual Christian work had been first thought, then spoken, in Greek. Plenty of remarkable Westerns were trying to put the Greek inheritance into Latin forms; but Augustine, man of astounding *interest* and *memory*, not only read everything he could lay hands on, but forgot none of it, and put it into magnificent Latin; he taught people not to be afraid, because they were Christian, of the best legacies of pagan days, and stands, literally, along with Anthony and Benedict, at the head of the whole series of schools that for centuries educated Europe, and of another series of masterpieces of literature and thought that without him never would have existed. Of course, later centuries developed and even corrected his ideas; but without those ideas, they might never have known so much as how to think.

I can single out but three points out of so very many that I could speak of in regard of St. Augustine. First, if there is one thing you prize it is your individual will, *strength* of will, not merely power of choosing. You know you are not machines, you bitterly resent being made to feel the slave of circumstance. Augustine, more than any one man, impressed upon the Christian world a doctrine of *will*-power—oh, not perhaps just the one you'd like! He, by the very intensity of his own life, displayed how strong the human will can be; but he experienced, and insisted, that the human will is itself but a weakling if not helped by God's Grace. Nay, there are certain things that our poor human will can never manage for itself—it can never force its way up into that supernatural love of God, union with God, happiness in God, that Grace does lift us to. He saw, therefore, two things—first, that you must work as hard as you can with that will-power that is in your God-given human nature; and also that you never can fully succeed without God's help. That is why it is so supremely important to pray. To keep in touch with God. To preserve contact. To get His Grace. 'Without Me,' said our Lord, 'you can do nothing.' We can do something, but nothing that gets us all the way through, and all the time. In the long run, the total difference is between the man who never prays and the man who does. The second point is this—He lived just when the thing that seemed *eternal*—the Roman Empire and its culture —seemed to be breaking up. The very name 'Vandal' has survived amongst us as indicating a man who has no sense of the very elements of decency, or of art, or of civilisation. The Vandals were one of the tribes of northerners who were at all points crashing their way into the Empire. Augustine himself could not see how anything whatsoever was to survive. To him it really did seem to be the end of the human world. And in those years he wrote his supreme work—*Civitas Dei*—the City, the State, the Civilisation of GOD. No upset that we are experiencing comes anywhere near what he was involved in. Neither money nor rank nor tradition, nor social or political framework of any sort, was surviving. Yet he lived through it, himself unbroken, saving his own period from complete collapse, making life possible for the future. He was able to do this, because he could hold firmly on to the Truths concerning God, and the human soul, and right and wrong, and their eternal consequences, and that one and only everlasting king, who is Christ, and the one imperishable kingdom, which is the Church, the Body whereof Christ is head. We are too often trying to do without these things; yet through them and in no other way comes salvation, civic, social, moral or supernatural. Without God and Christ, and vital contact with them through prayer and self-sacrifice, we ourselves will be vainly trying to build, yet once more, a new civilisation with the old materials.

Finally, Augustine has made himself felt, from one generation to another, *as a man*. Not only a man who seems to have experienced literally all that human man *can* experience, and to have transmitted it through that book, the *Confessions*, that must have been read more than any book in the world, save the Gospels and perhaps the Psalms, but who none the less made no chaos of his life, but gathered all those elements together into one splendid whole; because, ignorant of no human passion that we could possibly experience, he discarded nothing that was in himself, but gathered it, put order into it, and made it perfect, by directing it towards God who created it and alone can make the most and best of it. 'Thou hast made us for Thyself; and restless is our heart, till it finds rest in Thee.'

Augustine is spoken of from almost every point of view in *A Monument to St. Augustine* (Sheed and Ward).

Also *The Confessions of St. Augustine* and *An Augustine Synthesis*.

It was actually during the chaos that ensued that the great creative and immortal genius, St. Benedict, lived and died (480–543); that gigantic personalities like Popes St. Leo the Great, and St. Gregory the Great, ruled the Church (d. 461 and 604 respectively). Gregory must be called the supreme personality in the world of his period. And that scholarly and laborious man (like St. Isidore, d. 636) tried to transmit what could be saved from the wreck. Nor did missionary energy flag—St. Augustine of Canterbury (d. 604); St. Boniface (d. 755); St. Ansgar (d. 865)—to mention but a name or two from among those to whom our North has been ever since indebted; St. Patrick had died about 464; St. Aidan in 651; St. Columba in 597: and that sweetest figure, almost, in the whole of our history, St. Bede the Venerable, who died in 735, is quite simply to be called the 'Father of English History.' I mention these names all but haphazard, and only to recall that heroic figures are to be found in every century of the tormented adolescence of our Europe. Perhaps the years between 750 and 950 were the darkest, because of the violence of the period and the practical kidnapping of great positions in the Church by men who wished themselves to control that controlling power, and made their own base minions into prelates. It is during what some have thought the darkest hour that Hermann the Cripple, of whom I speak next, was born; though in reality that dark had never been at all complete; and already the dawn was breaking.

*

HERMANN THE CRIPPLE

'PAIN IS NOT UNHAPPINESS'

1013–1054

ST. AUGUSTINE died in 430, so that nearly six hundred years went by before Hermann of Reichenau, of whom I am going to speak, was born. Yet there is the queerest link between them—a book, written before the birth of Christ, by the pagan Roman Cicero, was read and re-read by St. Augustine, and was a favourite of the little cripple Hermann. And now it is lost. All *we* can do is to read scattered quotations from that book *Hortensius*, written two thousand years ago, which lit visions five hundred years later in the mind of the man who gave her new soul to Europe, and that was so precious, on his death-bed, to Hermann after another five hundred years.

On July 18th, 1013, a son was born to Wolfrad, Count of Altshausen in Swabia, and his wife Hiltrud. They belonged to gorgeous families, and noblemen, crusaders, and great prelates provide names that jostle one another in those pedigrees. Yet none of them do we remember, save the little fellow who was born most horribly deformed. He was afterwards nicknamed 'Contracted,' so hideously distorted was he; he could not stand, let alone walk; could hardly sit, even in the special chair they made for him; even his fingers were all but too weak and knotted for him to write; even his mouth and palate were deformed and he could hardly be understood when he spoke. In a pagan world he would, without argument, have been exposed, at birth, to perish; modern pagans, especially when they observe that he was one of fifteen children, would announce that he never should have been born; when they become still more logical, they will announce that such an abortion should be painlessly put out of the way. And twice over would they say so, when I tell you that he appeared, to the

40

judges of nine hundred years ago, to be what we would call Defective. What did these people, skulking in the murk of those 'Dark Ages' (as we have the steely nerve to call them) do ? They sent him to a monastery, and they prayed.

If you remember what I said about St. Anthony you will recall that it was monasteries that took over what they could from the ancient culture, and developed it. Into Germany, that culture came not only from the Latin South, but by way of England (St. Boniface of Devon) and most certainly from Ireland. But it was popular. The rather hard Latin culture was softened by charming elements from Germany. German translations of the gospels were appearing; German sermons were being preached; hardly a great name in Latin or Greek literature but became known in this way, and always, need I say, through those monasteries—like St. Gall, Fulda, Reichenau—that formed vast libraries, and also schools that moved about along with Emperors; indeed, Duke Bruno, brother of the Emperor Otto I, did not disdain to act as professor; and, you may say, every student also taught. Would that they did so, or could do so, now ! Let me just add that this was not a merely masculine culture. The nun Hrotswitha of Gaudesheim had Otto's niece for abbess and as instructress in the classics. Hrotswitha proceeded to write all sorts of literature, including comedies, one of which has been quite recently acted before an intensely interested audience in England.

To one such monastery the defective freak was sent. Reichenau was on a lovely little island in Lake Constance where the Rhine runs strong towards its cataracts. It had existed before Charlemagne—for some two hundred years, that is—by the high road on the shore opposite. Italian and Greek, Irish and Icelandic travellers passed to and fro. It sheltered famous scholars; it had its school of painting; tenth century paintings as at Oberzell, eleventh as at Niederzell, exist, made by monks with the heart, if not yet the hand, of Fra Angelico. Here the boy grew up. Here the lad that could hardly stammer with his tongue, found his mind developing under who knows what

manner of religious psycho-therapy ? Not once in his life can
he have been 'comfortable' or out of pain; yet what are the
adjectives that cluster round him ? I translate them from the
Latin biography. Pleasant, friendly, easy to talk to; always
laughing; never criticising; eagerly cheerful; trying as hard as
possible to be—ah ! here is a word I find difficult—to be
'thoroughly decent' would be, I think, our equivalent. And
the result was, that '*everybody loved him*.' And meanwhile the
courageous lad—never, remember, at his ease in a chair nor so
much as flat in bed—learnt mathematics, Greek, Latin,
Arabic, astronomy and music. He wrote a whole treatise upon
Astrolabes. I believe that you found the Equator, or measured
the height of the stars with astrolabes. . . . In his preface
he says: 'Hermann, the leastest of Christ's poor ones, and of
amateur philosophers the follower more slow than any
donkey, yes, than snail . . .' has been persuaded by the
prayers of 'numbers of my friends' (yes, 'everybody' liked
him) to write this scientific treatise. He'd keep wriggling out
of doing so, making all sorts of excuses, but really through his
'lumpish laziness'; but at long last he offered to the friend to
whom he dedicated his booklet at any rate the *theory* of the
thing, and said that if he liked it he would work it out in
practical detail later on.

And, would you believe it, with those twisted fingers the
indomitable lad *made* astrolabes, and also clocks and musical
instruments. Never conquered; never idle ! And as for
music—would that our modern choirs could read him ! He
says that a competent musician ought to be able to compose a
reasonable tune, or anyway to judge it, and *finally*, to sing it.
Most singers, says he, attend to the third point only, and
never *think*. They sing, or rather howl, not realising that no
one can sing properly if his thought is out of harmony with his
voice. To such songsters loud voice is everything. This is
worse than donkeys, who after all *do* make much more noise,
but never mix up braying with bellowing. No one tolerates,
says he, grammatical mistakes; yet the rules of grammar are
artificial, whereas 'music springs straight from Nature,' and
therein not only do men fail to correct their faults, but they

actually defend them. . . . The jolly little cripple could use, when he wanted to, a rather caustic tongue ! Yet it is practically certain that it was he who wrote the glorious hymn, *Salve Regina*, with its plain-chant melody, still used to-day all over the Catholic world, the *Alma Redemptoris*, and others. But besides this the active, vigorous brain of Hermann, who was not only in touch with every important family-tradition of that time, but in possession of many an ancient book now lost to us owing to the destruction of so many monastery libraries later on, wrote a *Chronicon*, or world-history from Christ's day to his own. Experts say that it was amazingly accurate, retailing, of course, tradition, yet objective and original. Here, then, you have the crippled monk in his cell, alert, eyes wide open to the outside world, yet never cynical, never cruel (so many sufferers grow cruel), but making a complete perspective of the currents of life in Europe.

Well, the time came to die. I leave his friend and historian Berthold to relate that. ' When at last the loving kindliness of God was deigning to free his holy soul from the tedious prison of this world, he was attacked by pleurisy, and for ten days was almost all the time in agony. At last, one day, very early in the morning, after Mass, I, whom he counted his closest friend, went and asked him if he felt a little better, "Do not ask me about that," he answered ; "not about *that* ! . . . Listen carefully. I shall certainly die very soon. I shall not live ; I shall not recover." And then he went on to say how during the night he had felt as if he were re-reading that *Hortensius* of Cicero's, with its wise sayings upon right and wrong, and all that he had himself meant to write upon the subject. "And under the strong inspiration of that reading, the whole of this present world and all that belongs to it—yes, this mortal life itself has become mean and wearisome, and on the other hand, the world to come, that shall not pass, and that eternal life, have become so unspeakably desirable and dear, that I hold all these passing things as light as thistledown. I am tired of living." ' Berthold, when Hermann spoke thus, broke down completely, and, says he, 'uttered agitated cries and kept no proper control of myself.' Hermann, after a while, 'quite indignantly upbraided me, trembling, and looking at me sideways with puzzled eyes. "Heart's beloved," said he; "Do not weep, do not weep for me."' And he made Berthold take his writing-tablets and put down a few last things. 'And,' he added, 'by remembering daily that you too are to die, prepare yourself with all your energy for the self-same journey, for, on some day and hour, you know not when, you shall follow me forth—me, your dear, dear friend.' And on these words, he ceased.

Hermann died, after receiving the Body and Blood of Christ in Holy Communion, among all his friends, on September 24th, and was buried—hidden little monk as he had been—amid 'great lamentation,' in his own estate of Altshausen that he had given up so long ago.

When I first came across this 'life' in a crabbed old Latin book at Oxford, I felt as if a wave of sweetest air were turning a stuffy room into freshness and fragrance. For the written Life is so very much alive—Hermann *lives* so vividly! Not just because he could write on the theory of music or mathematics, could compile laborious histories and knew so many languages, but because of his *pluck*, his fineness of soul, his gaiety in pain, his readiness to chaff and answer back, the sweetness of mood that made him 'loved by all.' And I beg of you to stand no nonsense from those who suggest that a sickly body produces a sickly mind, that it is on physical heftiness, body-breeding, that we should concentrate if we would have good citizens, or that physical well-being, though desirable, is in any sense whatsoever necessary for happiness. Vulgarest confusion of mind with nerves! Hardly one of those pedigrees of sickly and criminal families is worth anything at all. Hardly ever have the effects of environment upon the child or descendant of, say, two criminals, been disentangled from what is assumed to be their heredity. You are safe in doubting whether mental or moral characteristics *ever* are inherited. Proper bodily upbringing plays certainly its great but perfectly subordinate part; proper training for the mind plays a primary and enormous one—and this, believe me, must include as paramount two things—love and religion—and the two are intertwined. And in this twisted little fellow from the Dark Ages shines out the triumph of the Faith that inspired love, of the love that acted loyally by Faith, and Hermann provides the proof of how Pain does not spell Misery, nor Pleasure, Happiness.

The next Saint I have chosen to speak of was Edward, king and 'confessor,' first, because I wanted to introduce an Englishman into this series; and then, because he stands as symbol of an idea—of what is meant by legitimate human 'king-ship.' This series is not meant, exactly, or at all, to 'broadcast' ideas, however just; but to exhibit some human histories in the hopes, please God, that what is meant by 'Sanctity' may emerge from them. However, it is quite reasonable to exhibit also certain types or general principles, with which all such histories will be seen essentially to clash. First, you have the Individualist, who lives for Self alone. The Saint is alien quite from him. You have the man who devotes himself to 'class'—who lives, or works, in enmity towards some other class. It makes not the slightest difference whether he be a rich man exploiting the working-class, or a poor man hating and enflaming anger against a wealthier or more human-wise powerful 'class.' This hate, this exploitation, are equally antagonistic to Christianity, let alone to Sanctity. There is also the man who is a Nationalist, by which I mean, he who hates any country (let alone race) other than his own, either because he has suffered from it, or fears it, or despises it; or even, he who seeks to aggrandise his own country, as such, by exploiting any other country, or race. Finally, there is the man who places the State above Christ, Cæsar above God, and who, if he possesses the power, treats the Citizen as existing for the State, not (as is the truth) the State for the better-being of the Citizen. Beyond this Tyranny cannot go. Self-Worship can find no more ultimate an expression. The opposite to this notion was enshrined in St. Edward, king; and in his contemporary, St. Stephen, king of Hungary.

*

ST. EDWARD, KING OF ENGLAND

'KINGSHIP IS NOT CÆSARISM'

1003–1066

I FIRST thought of speaking of him one Sunday when I had to go straight from Westminster Cathedral, close to the abbey that we owe to Edward, to a church in Chiswick, also dedicated in his honour and packed out with people observing his feast-day. When I re-read all I could find about St. Edward I half regretted my choice, for not much that is picturesque is recorded about his character. On third thoughts, I decided that after all there was something worth saying just because it would not be so very dramatic. And when I remembered the names of much fiercer, more spectacular, men who surrounded him—it amused me once more to doubt whether even one in those churches was called Sweyn, Thurkill, let alone Hardicanute, whereas there must have been dozens of Edwards, Neds or Teds, present; and all our kings named Edward have inherited their name from that distant monarch who, till forty, lived in exile.

I am certainly not going to make a history-lecture here. Suffice it to say that after the splendid reign of Alfred you might have thought that this country would have thriven. He died in 901, bequeathing freedom in his very Will. 'For God's love, and for the benefit of my soul, I will that they be masters of their own freedom and of their own choice; and in the name of the Living God, I entreat that no man disturb them by extraction of money or in any other way, but that they may be left free to serve any lord they may choose.' As a matter of fact, the land went back to misery. The rivalries of great personages or families, and nationalistic greed, Saxon, Angle, Swede, Dane, at one another's throats, brought our island into a state of ravage and burnings, of murder, hamstringing, blinding, scalping which have been described as 'hardly paralleled in the annals of American (Indian) ferocity,' and, I might add, to incests and allied horrors *not* to be paralleled among just savages. You hardly wonder that force, indeed, extreme severity, were *demanded* from those who cared or were responsible for justice; and the critics who half-sneer at Edward for his gentleness ought at least not to abuse kings, judges or bishops if, to repress the paroxysms of outrage, they used stern methods that he did not. Yet, after all . . . his is the personality that survives!

When the Danish Canute was acknowledged in 1017 to be King of all England, which thereupon became part of the Scandinavian empire, he sent away the infant sons of the previous king, Edmund Ironside, to Hungary. King Stephen in Hungary was himself a saint; and of his work, enduring till our own period and the treaty of Versailles, and destined to be revived, I should have liked to speak. Edmund's half-brothers, Alfred and Edward, had been taken away to Normandy. But at Canute's death, his two sons, Harold and Hardicanute, again tore the land in half; the former died after four years; the latter, after two years' reign, had a fit during an orgy and died too. It was 1042. Someone had to be king, and so Edward was sent for, because he was the only survivor of the exiled brothers—Alfred had previously made an attempt to regain his crown, but Harold had caught him, massacred his followers and sent the wretched prince, tied naked to a horse, exhibited like a monstrosity through the villages, to Ely, where his eyes were put out and he died.

Now reflect that Edward had grown up a quiet man, robust and ruddy-faced, but with hair and beard early enough quite white, liking the hunt and hawking, but also a home-lover; English by descent, no doubt, but convinced (no wonder) of the immense superiority of Norman culture; and take note that an exceptional amount of agricultural and atmospheric depression distressed much of his reign, and that there were actually earthquakes causing much alarm at, for example, Derby and Worcester; while the great lords at home and threats from overseas kept the horizon seemingly as black as ever—you might have thought that such a man in such circumstances would never have emerged into the light of history at all. Yet he, more than any of them, *did*. The real point is, that even if official historians glorified his reign, partly because it was an *English* one between the Danish tyranny and the Norman invasion and conquest, *public opinion* seldom goes simultaneously wrong about *Character; public affection* is not lightly given, or at least, if lightly given, does not last. But when Edward died, his people simply worshipped him, and it was to the 'laws and customs of the good king Edward' that they constantly and successfully appealed, thereafter, against Norman oppression. Why was this ? I consider, wholly because of the man's character, formed, not by self-indulgence —that *forms* nothing—but by deliberate unselfishness. He was a true king, precisely because he lived, not for himself, but for his people. No doubt he might have kept some of the great earls in order at the expense of massacring others, but he did not adopt this policy. He could, perhaps, have yielded to foreign petitions to enter into wars of aggrandisement; but into one only foreign war did he enter—a war of justice, on behalf of Malcolm, son of the Scottish Duncan, whom Macbeth in 1039 had murdered. And again, how strange it seems that we remember Edward, not because of this war, but in spite of it; and not one of us might so much as have heard of Macbeth, had not Shakespeare been inspired to enshrine some shreds of his story in a work of superb imagination. Millions must have read 'Macbeth' without feeling—without so much as dreaming—that the tragic king was ever a real person. But Edward stands out so solid, so brilliant, so alive !¹

In that age when extortion and bribery played so massive a part, Edward seemed indifferent to money—he remitted the whole of the Dane-geld that had been exacted during thirty-eight years from the people and formed a great part of his personal revenue; when his nobles, anxious for his favour, had squeezed from their vassals a large sum and offered it to him, he refused it, and ordered it to be restored to those who had

---

[1] Not everyone agrees with this estimate of Macbeth. We can safely say that the little war could not but seem just to Edward.

paid it in. Edward was, I should suppose, often enough cheated by men whom he trusted too much; but his ideal was ever *Justice*, national and personal. Thus when Pope Leo IX in 1049 consecrated the cathedral of Rheims and held a council there, Edward sent a Bishop and two Abbots to bring back his decrees 'for the welfare of Christendom,' and again sent two Bishops to the larger council in Rome, as representing the Anglo-Saxon hierarchy and as his own petitioners. The results have been curious and endure. Not only did they bring back stringent enactments concerning men who, by means of bribes, should seek to obtain bishoprics or abbacies, but, an answer to an anxiety of Edward's private conscience. In those times of united Christendom, all eyes turned naturally to Rome. Edward had made a vow to go there. When he became king his nobles dreaded his leaving the kingdom to the probability of renewed civil strife in his absence. The Pope understood this; dispensed him from his vow; but asked that anything Edward had collected for his journey should be given to the poor, and that he should found, or restore, an abbey dedicated to St. Peter. Thenceforward, Edward annually set aside one-tenth of the revenues of his manois, and finally re-built, or rather built, Westminster Abbey. Later kings, and very ill-inspired architects, have since then added pieces to that edifice (like the two poor little towers); but the main glory of the work is due to Edward and Pope Leo. It is pathetic that in 1065 he went to London on purpose to witness its dedication; on Christmas Eve he was attacked by fever; with his habitual self-control he tried to remain as cheerful as ever, presided at all functions, instructed his wife Edith to see to the due decoration of the church. But on December 28th she had to represent him at the actual ceremony in the place of which Aeldred, Archbishop of York, when visiting Rome for the Archbishop's pallium, in 1063, had obtained so many privileges and whither papal legates had come to confirm them. Edward died on January 5th, 1066, and because of our fantastic habit of beginning to learn English history from the latter part, only, of that year, Edward, with so much more, has subsided into being a mere 'pre-conquest' monarch. He was buried in the abbey. The eleventh century Bayeux tapestry depicts the scene; his shrine, having survived later attacks upon it, was once more enriched by King Edward VII and other members of the present royal family, and is still surrounded by kneeling pilgrims on October 13th, the day when St. Thomas à Becket, in the presence of King Henry II, solemnly removed St. Edward's body to the shrine itself.

The Christian, as you know, is not committed by his Christianity to any special system of government, be it by king or cabinet or president. But as St. Paul bequeathed more to England and to the world than a cathedral and its dome, so Edward left better behind him than his abbey. He enshrined in himself and exhibited to the world the two essential elements of right authority—the truths that all authority descends ultimately from God; and that all government exists for the well-being of the governed, not of itself. Christianity commits the Christian to no form of government as essentially better than any other—monarchy, presidency, dictatorship, cabinet-government, popular government, or any other sort; the Christian, objecting as indeed he must to anarchy, demands *government*, but not (save by reason of purely personal preference) this sort or that. On the other hand, he knows that political life, like social, artistic, moral, familiar—every kind or department of life, has to recognise GOD as sole ultimate source of Power, and the Christian must be able to be obeying God when obeying the mandates of his prince. To fail to remember this is to begin to offer to Cæsar what belongs to God, and to worship the Beast and his Image, to adore what is fain to set itself up (as the Scriptures so often say) in the Holy Place itself above all that can *deserve* the Name of God. No State, no Government, is Absolute over Conscience. And all authority whether in the home, or in shop or firm, business or trading concern, regional, national, racial matters, exists by no manner of means for the sake of those who are the possessors and wielders of that authority. No boss has the right to exploit one single man, whether yellow, white or black. Yet every age, our own included, has tended to produce its own version of tyranny, and of slave-trade. Government must rule, but never may be Tyrant; the governed must obey, but must never be enslaved. May those principles of obedience to God, and so, of Justice towards man, which made Edward into a king who also was a saint, remain. His palaces have perished; not so his abbey. May what it symbolised survive, be intensified amongst us, and where need be, restored, else lost for us will be that righteous rule which is an image upon earth of God's own kingdom. May that Kingdom come, fully and lastingly.

The constellation of Saints belonging to the Middle Ages is too great to enable me in any way to enumerate them. Best to state simply this—as from about A.D. 1000 the real 'Reformation' began. It began with men like St. Peter Damian (d. 1072); St. Romuald (d. 1027); and passed through the magnificent St. Bruno, founder of the Carthusians (d. 1101), St. Anselm, Archbishop of Canterbury (d.1109), St. Bernard of Clairvaux, of whom I regret so much not to have spoken— by far the greatest man in Europe of his time—preacher of Crusades, theologian, and probably the author of *Iesu dulcis memoria:* 'Jesus, the very thought of Thee . . .' (d. 1153), St. Thomas à Becket (martyred 1170), into the century of St. Francis and St. Dominic. I speak next of the former of these two (who could omit him ?); and then, lest I seem to neglect the latter, of his wonderful 'descendant,' Thomas of Aquino. For this is what human nature does. . . . The great Event provokes the intense Passion, and along with the passion (we may hope), the Poet. But the passion cools; then comes the man who wants to tell you just what happened—the Historian. And then the man follows who reflects upon the facts—the Philosopher. Just as the war between Greece and Persia was followed by the great Tragedians, and these by a Herodotus, a Thucydides, so they in their turn were followed by a Plato and an Aristotle. Sometimes the process is speeded up—Francis and Dominic had their historians, but almost at once appeared the great philosophers, St. Bonaventura in the one case (d. 1274), and St. Thomas (d. also 1274). No period more than this (save perhaps the next and most seemingly disastrous one) overwhelms me with the sense of the glorious sweep and progress of the Church's Wisdom, and of her Holiness.

*

ST. FRANCIS OF ASSISI

THE 'POOR LITTLE MAN' OF CHRIST

1182–1226

So recklessly are the words 'dark ages', 'medieval' and so forth chucked about, that I venture to make clear that the *only* 'medieval' Saints I speak of in this series are St. Francis of Assisi, to-day, and St. Thomas Aquinas, please God, next Sunday. If anyone wants to use the—to my mind—clumsy misnomer: The Dark Ages, he should confine it to the period between, say, 750 and 950; the medieval period can be regarded as extending from 1050 to 1350, and that is a generous allowance. Saints Paul, Anthony and Augustine belonged neither to the dark, not to the medieval periods; Hermann the Cripple and St. Edward were in a transitional period working up to the medieval world. Francis and Thomas are genuine medievals; and other tickets will have to be found for anyone to be mentioned after them. It is true that the 'Dark Ages' can so be named largely because we have, till recently, studied them hardly at all: everybody is aware how completely many a man's estimate of the Middle Ages has had to be revised, since modern scholarship has concentrated on that period. The theory of unbroken human progress has long ago collapsed. In very many ways the thirteenth century was immeasurably ahead of either the sixteenth or the eighteenth; and the world-wide study devoted to the history of St. Francis, and the almost passionate affection in men of the most various creeds that his personality inspires, have contributed more than almost anything to place his supremely creative century in its right perspective.

Francis appears abruptly, aged about twenty, taken prisoner in a war between Umbrian Assisi and her rival town, Perugia. It was the stormy period of transition from the rule of the great lord in his castle, to that of the cities and their citizens, and such little wars were frequent. Francis was son of a very wealthy merchant; his father adored him, and indulged—nay gloried in—the lad's rocketing career. Francis, recklessly extravagant, yet lavish to beggars no less than in his dress; daring and original to the point of the fantastic; small in frame but utterly untiring, almost ecstatically responsive to music and to colour, yet with an artist's swift reactions towards melancholy and dream; Italian through and through, yet fascinated by French poetry and the chivalrous tales related by the troubadours, Francis was acknowledged leader of the young men of his city, was always chosen 'master' of their 'revels,' was acquainted with every form of licence. And yet, unless I err, he was saved from *committing* himself to what he mixed with by that glamorous romantic veil that made him *need* to transpose even war, even love, even dress, into a semi-mystical world of the imagination. After his capture and imprisonment, during which he was so gay that his fellow-captives thought him half-delirious, reaction came. Liberated, but weak, he stood leaning on a stick staring at the cypresses and vineyards of that gold-misted world and wondered that ever he had so much loved them. . . . But the old spirit in part revived. He set out on another war, against invading Germans. Then, having dreamed of a palace, full of splendid armour, where a bride awaited him . . . he, half asleep, heard himself asked: 'Which is better—to serve the servant, or to serve the Lord?' 'Of course, to serve the Lord!' 'Why, then, make a master of the servant . . .?' Half-dazed, he returned to Assisi; resumed his mastership of revels, but would sit abruptly abstracted in the middle of the feasts. He had suddenly noticed Poverty—the frightful poverty of the Assisi underworld which stole out from its black squalor to gaze at these golden lads. . . . His companions chaffed him, and asked him if he was in love. . . . Yes, and with a princess more noble, more lovely, than any that they knew. They guffawed; but it remained that he had caught sight of Poverty and had begun to love her. To love her, even while his very soul crept with horror at the idea of embracing her. . . . He began to pray. He pilgrimaged to Rome and not only poured out what money he had upon the destitute, but made a beggar of himself for one day and returned to Assisi still sick at memory of the rags, the filth, the stench, the humiliation. He felt he must conquer that—slowly. Well, at least he would no more do his alms in secret, terrorised by the idea of the mockery of his own 'class'; he gave them publicly at his own door. Not enough ! not deep-biting enough, because still the act as of one who stood above, done towards men who crouched beneath him. He must *equalise* himself ! He met a leper, and beating down his loathing, kissed the hand into which he placed his gift. And the leper lifted his face and gave, in his turn, to Francis the kiss of peace. . . . The decisive step, unconsciously, had been taken. For awhile he stumbled around his new domain of Poverty. He saw a ruined chapel, San Damiano. He had heard a voice : 'Francis, restore My Church, which is falling into ruins.' Losing for a moment all perspective, he sold a lot of his father's merchandise and carried the proceeds to the S. Damiano priest. The poor man was terrified, and refused it. Francis's father was furious, seized him, beat him, imprisoned him, and in the long run renounced his son, even as that son now renounced the whole of the life to which he had been educated.

Since in a quarter of an hour's talk I have to leave out almost everything, let me insist on this. You will never understand Francis till you realise that with all the love and loyalty of his heart he *married Poverty for Christ's sake*. He regarded Poverty not only as no disgrace but as a glory. She was the Princess Poverty. To pay court to Money, to devote your life to Money, to engage yourself to Money, *that* was the illusion in any case : to do so with your eyes open, *that* was the apostasy and the degradation. And this, not merely because he saw in a philosophical sort of way that the free man, the really rich man, was the man who cared nothing for coins— even the pagans had seen that : the Stoic, the Cynic, the Buddhist, have seen it very clearly. Nor did he become poor just because in a philanthropic sort of way he was sorry for poor people—poor people often resent that sort of com- miseration most bitterly.

No. The point is that Francis saw the Truth that no man may be assessed according to what he *has*, but according to what he *is;* and he is, what *God* sees him to be; and God esteems him entirely according to his Christlikeness; and Francis found himself becoming 'poor' just in proportion as he became like Christ. Christ, 'being rich, for our sakes made Himself poor'; 'even Christ pleased not Himself.' People to-day are poorer than they were—but reluctantly, kicking against it. I get letter after letter from America, from New Zealand, from Australia, and now from South Africa, lamenting that so little work, and therefore money, is to be got. Men pray for the re-building of trade—the chance to make a fortune. They want to build the social edifice over again, BUT, out of the same materials, on the same architectural principles. Impossible. And thank God for it. Money-getting, money-having, money spendable upon self—no life can thus be made. 'Standard of Life' is a term endlessly repeated nowadays. It used to be reckoned in terms of motor-cars and cinemas, and 'having a good time.' Hopeless. All that has to be turned upside down. 'Standard of Life' is a spiritual thing. The standard of an unjust millionaire's life is lower than that of the honourable scullion on whose head he plants his gold-shod hoof. Francis saw that; Christ taught that; and such is the verdict, in eternity, of God.

If this is realised, I hardly care what else I omit. I cannot speak of the gradual grouping of thousands upon thousands of men around St. Francis; the formation of his Order, and of its outer ring, so to say, the Third Order; nor of the exquisite idyll of St. Clare and the making of the Second Order, composed of those 'Poor Clares' of whom we have so many in England, thank God, and whose history has always been one of perfect fidelity to perfect poverty. Nor can I explain the slow, prudent hesitating and finally most definite approbation obtained from Rome for all of this; nor the Saint's expeditions outside Italy, even to the Sultan's camps in Egypt. I shall not, on the one hand, describe his bitter disappointments when he realised (as only his sweet simplicity could have failed to do) that the mass of his followers could not possibly burn with his pure flame, nor love poverty and the cross as he did; nor yet shall I trace the thousand streams of art, drama, song, social and missionary and educational work that have flowed through the world because of St. Francis. Cut out what was due to Francis in the work of Dante, and Giotto; in philosophic and scientific areas, in the work of Duns Scotus or Roger Bacon or St. Bonaventura; in the realm of government, men like St. Louis of France; of charity, women like Queen St. Elizabeth of Hungary, who, like Dante, were members of his Third Order, and what an infinity will you lose ! And what, when we recall that in the sheer history of electricity itself, Galvani, Volta, and Ampère were all members of that same Third Order ! Why, I must omit even that unique gem of literature, the Little Flowers of St. Francis, and no more than mention his own Canticle of the Sun, wherein he finds all nature—Brother Wind, the air and clouds and fair and every sort of weather; Sister Water, so helpful and humble and precious and pure; Brother Fire, gay, strong, lighting up the dark—found all these to be, in *their* way, his brothers and sisters, no less than those human men and women who in their far *better way* 'for Thy love, Lord, forgive and are weak and are troubled and in peace endure—for by Thee, Lord, shall they be crowned.' And before he died, he added: 'Praised be my Lord for our Sister, bodily death, from which no man may flee that liveth. . . . Praise ye and bless my Lord and give Him thanks, and be subject to Him with great humility !' But what it were a scandal and a shame for me to omit, were at least an allusion to that miracle which reproduced in his very flesh the external semblance of the death of Jesus Christ. In the year 1224, in the year and indeed the month and almost on the very day when the first Friars were landing here in England at Dover, Francis went up into the precipitous rocks of Mount Alvernia to pray in solitude. There it was that, during an ecstasy, he found the likeness of the wounds of Christ impressed upon his hands and feet and side. No one now doubts, or should doubt, of the historical character of this event. Concerning the mechanics of its physio-psychology, so to speak, experts still dispute, and by all means let them do so.

Let instances be quoted of how a mother's love has caused to appear on her own body marks suited to the accident that she helplessly witnessed happening to her child. We are grateful for such proofs of what an overwhelming, penetrating, soaring and seraphic love can bring about. But what is to be said of the love lit up within the heart of a man such, that not only it unites his spirit even here on earth in unsurpassable intensity and purity with Christ, but overflows upon his very body—or rather, what do I mean by that 'not only'? The true point is that not merely in the poor flesh of Francis were the marks of nails and lance anguishingly and accurately reproduced—a portent, without doubt—but that in his soul, so far as human soul can admit and support a love that is divine, the very love of Christ who lived and died for us, was reproduced. I have spoken, then, of Francis, and alas! have said hardly anything to convey to you what he was, but only, so to say, the two poles of his existence—the negative one, which means his rejection of all that human nature tends to make a god of; and his adherence with the very stuff of his soul to the GOD revealed in Jesus Christ, which is the positive definition of the life of Francis. He is not the elegant statuette that you perceive in artistic boudoirs; he is not the sweetly romantic preacher to the birds and the fish; he is not just the knight-errant of his Lord, wandering through the loveliness of Umbria; nor even, merely he who blessed Assisi from the hillside, as he approached it to die there, not seeing it, for tears and sickness had made his eyes go blind—and breaking bread into little pieces, for the last time, that he too might have, with his beloved, his final Supper, and dying on the ground just as the sun set and a myriad larks thrilled through the evening sky their happy hymn. Francis, having lived in this world and having so well understood us men, who must needs live within it, was himself not of it—no, he was not of it; and as for me, whose paganised youth he, more than any Saint, regenerated, I am glad, by the words of my lips, to have kissed, on my behalf and yours, the footsteps of his memory.

ST. THOMAS AQUINAS

THE 'DUMB OX': THE 'WORLD'S TUTOR'

1225(7?)–1274

THERE is a real pleasure in passing immediately from St. Francis of Assisi, so simple, so gay, so all that is the opposite of 'bookish,' who has won the love of the world, to St. Thomas of Aquino, in Southern Italy, who with positively startling rapidity is regaining its homage, as having been perhaps the most commanding intelligence that Europe ever produced. I will first very briefly summarise his life. His ancestry was superb; through his father, Count of Aquino, and his mother, Countess of Teano, he was related to the Emperors Henry VI and Frederick II, and to the kings of France, Castile and Aragon. At five, he was sent to school with the Benedictines of Monte Cassino. Later, he went to the University of Naples— his intelligence had already revealed itself such that *not* to have left monastery for university would have seemed a crime. Here, far from yielding to that insidious climate and the corruptions that surrounded him, he resolved to become a Dominican friar, and his superiors sent him to Rome in view of yet further journeys to the great centre of learning, Cologne, and the supreme focus of scientific study, Paris. But his parents indignant that the lad should renounce the pomps of his heredity for the black and white dress of the Dominicans, literally kidnapped and imprisoned him, and his brothers made the vilest attempts to destroy his chastity. Herein he conquered, and, managing to get books, filled his two years' imprisonment with intensive study. Finally, he reached Cologne and was put under Albertus Magnus a man of encyclopædic knowledge. At first Thomas listened so much and said so little that they called him the 'Dumb Ox.' But Albert said that his voice would one day fill the world; and indeed Thomas was to eclipse his master, at least in accuracy of observation and force of argument, and, merciful endowment, terseness of statement. Ordained priest about 1250, and equipped with one University degree after another, he moved to and fro among the great intellectual centres of the period, especially in Italy and France, but in 1263 he was present at a Dominican general chapter in London, and his tall, burly, upright figure has been seen at Blackfriars by the Thames, and he may have actually fingered the ancient stones that not along ago were transported thence to their proper place to-day—the Dominican Priory at Haverstock Hill. It seems humanwise inexplicable how, during these years of continuous travel and teaching, yes, and of preaching and apostolic work, he can not only have produced his enormous literary output, but have *thought* the firm-woven texture of philosophy that his books contain, let alone have studied the authorities he uses and quotes, especially as during his last years he manifested an ever-increasing distaste for that sort of human knowledge and love for the understanding that comes through direct communication with God. And observe, that when he died, in 1274, in a Cistercian monastery, having endeavoured to obey the Pope's mandate that he should go to the great Council of Lyons, he was not yet fifty!

Now, when I say that probably no one man has so influenced human thought as St. Thomas has, I may seem to you to be talking nonsense. Yet thinkers have thriven just in proportion as even unconsciously they obeyed his principles of thought, and have done flimsy work in proportion as they have scorned, or just not known of, the intellectual method that he brought to such perfection. But only within the last, say, forty years has his name, and has the whole character of his period begun to come back into their proper place in men's appreciation. For it was the fashion to suppose that no one had thought or said anything worth anything till the sixteenth, or, indeed, till the nineteenth century. That fantastic balloon has been pricked and the conceited air let out of it. Not only was the thirteenth century the time when practically all Europe's universities either came into being, or received their rapid development; not only was it the time of—on the one hand—the most intensive study of sheer *fact* (in Albertus Magnus, for example, and in his two pupils, Roger Bacon and Thomas Aquinas, you will find all that should have led up swiftly to an applied knowledge of high explosives, of lenses, and of internal combustion engines, and again, a perfect knowledge of the 'sex' of plànts and of such exquisitely subtle observations as the evaporation of sap through their cuticles)—but also of the boldest practical theorising, connected for example, with the correction of the calendar based partly on the knowledge of the time taken by light to travel, and so forth. It was the period, again, of artistic development and of literary origins—it was then that the legend of King Arthur, the Romaunt de la Rose, the Golden Legend, the Nibelungenlied, and more still, took shape, which have influenced literature ever since; not to speak of the great developments in Law, in Guild-Life, in sheer exploration with consequent knowledge of geography, and it was then (as I hope to mention when speaking of St. Camillus de Lellis) that the very creation or development of hospitals still surviving occurred—St. Thomas's, Bart's, etc.—and that a medical and surgical knowledge existed that later generations *forgot*.

And notice that the full education of the day was at the disposal of nearly everyone. Never has education been so 'democratic' since then. An enormously higher percentage of the population then went to universities than goes now or can possibly hope to go. Not that this cost them nothing. Personally, I think that little tends so swiftly and directly to degrade intellectual ambition as free education. Anyhow, in St. Thomas's day when education really was esteemed, enormous sacrifices were made by students and their friends for the sake of learning. Scholarships, burses, collections of all sorts were made, to get the would-be student actually to the university, to supply him with his books, and very food; he, on his side, was willing half the time to go without most of life's necessities and all its luxuries, and to earn his very keep not only by manual work outside of school-terms, so to say, as is nobly and inspiritingly done by so many young students in the United States to-day, but, by working within the Universities themselves during term, serving, for example, the professors and even their fellow-students.

Therefore, had St. Thomas put his tremendous influence and intellectual energy at the disposal of his age alone, his work would have been wide, deep and lasting. But he made a new gift to that world, which has assisted human thought ever since and could assist it at the present moment far more even than it does, were it better used. The great Greek thinker Aristotle had reached our thirteenth century in small fragments only of his works, ill-translated, and mostly by way of Arab and Jewish authors, who had made current very distorted versions of Aristotle's meaning, so much so, that the very name of that philosopher was suspected and disliked. St. Thomas, practically single-handed, turned the whole of this situation once and for all upside down. He caused, with the help of the Holy See, a complete and proper translation to be made; he explained the whole system of Aristotle more perfectly then ever yet it had been set forth; and he displayed the fact that, far from being of necessity, or at all, hostile to the Christian Faith, the tremendous treasures of antiquity could be brought into glad and free co-operation with the teachings of Christ. This in itself is an enormous benefit, because it can preserve religion from the miasma of sentimentalism that infects so much of it to-day. Do not imagine it is easy to think properly. It is far harder than learning about aeroplanes, or hunting, or making films. It is an *art*. And, it is very tiring. People seize every chance of not thinking, and end by half arguing you ought not to think, anyway in religion, but just to feel or to be what they dub 'mystical.'

Our popular press almost takes it for granted that nothing is to be known for certain, by means of the intelligence, of God, of the soul, of right and wrong; that in some vague way religion won't bear thinking about too closely; that history, and scientific research are, no one quite knows how, yet in their very nature hostile to religion. So the average man himself, hard-headed enough, accurate and precise, when, say, business is in hand, permits himself an incredible looseness of talk when spiritual things are concerned. Yet I suppose that nowhere in the world—no, not in Aristotle himself—will you find such ruthless distinction between speculation and proof, hypothesis and demonstration, such relentless logic as in St. Thomas, such laborious accumulation of all available fact, such shifting and reshifting and assessment of evidence, such absolute freedom from the scientific or philosophic fashion of the moment—for science has fads and fashions, slogans and cant-phrases too. Indeed, just now men of science (anxious to put science itself at the disposal of the multitude) are showing (to my mind) a recklessness of statement, indulging in an irresponsible guessing-in-public so second-rate as to be worse (because due to a vulgar affection for publicity and sensationalism) than the days of Tyndall and Huxley, even, witnessed, for these had a kind of crude, boyish harsh optimism about them which absolves them from much that was precipitate and has had to be abandoned. No; Aquinas read everything, and forgot nothing; never mixed up the materials with which he was dealing, whether they concerned sheer history, or human psychology (as when he treats of human passions, or of perfectly concrete matters like the effect of hot baths upon the mind . . .), or asceticism, or metaphysics, or revealed dogma and theology. Nowhere in his enormous work is the least dislocation to be found; nowhere a word used without its meaning having been previously made clear; nowhere a side-slip in an argument. We dare not say we have exhausted our understanding of any ancient philosopher whomsoever, till we see what his thoughts would have issued into by the time of, under the treatment of, St. Thomas; nor can we possibly do better, when reading any author later in date than St. Thomas, than to drive what he may write through the fine mesh of Thomas's own thought.

You are probably saying by now: 'What on earth has this talk been about? Who cares twopence whether Thomas Aquinas was or wasn't a great thinker? And if he was, what has that got to do with being a saint? And we are supposed to be listening, on these afternoons, to talks about *Saints*. That is bad enough. But if we don't get even that, but mere

talks about philosophers . . . well, we shall switch off !'
Do so, if you want to. But, well, St. Francis sufficed, all by
himself, to prove that a man can turn right upside down the
ordinary belief that Money is what man wants, and that his
proper job in life is (as an American millionaire once said to
me, with eyes wide open like a baby's with astonishment that
I could suppose anything else) *making dollars*, whereas hardly
a man knows the name of, and not one man remembers with
esteem or affection, any of the rich men of Francis's day,
while millions still love *him* with all their hearts. And Thomas
Aquinas suffices (had he not had a single disciple instead of
one generation after another of them) to upset the myth that
Religion fears Thought, fears Science, is an affair of emotion,
obscure tradition, of leaps in the dark, or even identical
with mystical union with God—though this, when genuine, is
a very sublime outcome of it. St. Thomas in his own person,
in his books, in the thousands of books written about him,
through the great Dominican Order to which he belonged, in
the schools that still live, think, and develop by means of his
impetus and method, disproves that myth. Religion does not
fear Enquiry, but courts it; nay, is the first to apply it—I have
never read any attacks on religion so drastic as those invented
by Aquinas ! But it was *not* just his intelligence that made
St. Thomas a *Saint*. He thought singularly lightly of the
intellectual side of his work. It is pathetic still to see his own
manuscript of one of his greatest books, preserved in the
Vatican Library, and to perceive how through paragraph after
paragraph of abbreviated, almost shorthand script, his pen
has drawn a line of yellowing ink, showing how dissatisfied
he was with what we find so treasurable. His extreme humility,
no doubt—like that, indeed, of any really great scholar—
made him think but poorly of his work; any such man sees
how tremendous is Truth, that the most of what man can
know of it is but little. But deeper still, he had come to live
in so habitual a communion with God, actually in the country
whereof the most accurate theology is but the map, that, said
he, 'all I have written now seems to me but of little value.'
This man of many travels, of intimate understanding of his

fellow-men, was, through his love for Jesus Christ, in such close touch with God, that all life, let alone all knowledge, had become for him a means of a holiest Communion; and perhaps the best way of entering into contact with St. Thomas is through his Eucharistic hymns, fragments of two of which, *O Salutaris* and *Tantum Ergo*, are sung Sunday by Sunday by millions still to-day.

Maritain's *St. Thomas Aquinas* (Sheed & Ward).

Saints seem to come into existence either when circumstances are very favourable, as in the second or the thirteenth centuries; or, when they are the reverse, as (perhaps) in the fourth and fifth or tenth; and certainly, at the time of the Renaissance. What happened at the Renaissance was practically this—after the 'Latin' renaissance came the 'Greek' one. People began to read Greek again, and were intoxicated by Greek beauty, and began in consequence to adopt Greek ideas and *principles*. These were of course pagan; whereas, however lawless men may have been in the Middle Ages, the background of their mind was Christian. This brought about the glorification of what was *merely* human, of the Body, and of the Intellect. Inevitably, the worship of the body, paid to it by men who could afford to spend money upon it, led to unthinkable misery among those who were poor and became ever poorer; and also, to contempt for the miserable Many on the part of the wealthy and luxurious Few. And the worship of the human intellect led, as always, to scepticism. Besides this, Nationalism was becoming an endemic plague in Europe; and it was now that was formulated the catch-phrase: '*Cuius regio, eius religio*'—'Faith depends on Frontiers.' Hence those 'Wars of Religion,' so-called. For these were not really any such things; but, Princes could use religion, or religious passions, as leverage for the mobilising of their peoples. Perhaps, since the aftermath of the Barbarian invasions, when Europe was beginning to form itself into some sort of order out of chaos—and the chaotic elements like powerful barons, disliked this very much and resisted it as much as they could—there has seldom been so much happiness and wrong-doing in our West. This is the moment when Saints began to appear far too numerous for me to make any attempt so much as to classify them, let alone to name them.

I have therefore chosen men who represent various categories, but tending all of them in the direction of philanthropy, provided always that word be used Christian-wise, as indicating love and service of one's fellow-men for Christ's sake. And also, men whose own spirit, and whose spiritual progeny, had nothing whatsoever to do with frontiers or politics, or even race. There will be no worship of the body in a Camillus, a Claver, or a Vincent de Paul, who did (and in their spiritual descendants still do) such an enormous work for the relieving of sheer pain: and certainly, the 'Red Cross,' which (though it does not know it) was anticipated by and in a true sense owes its existence to Camillus, is super-national; and so are the Societies that owe their origin to, or hold their title from a St. Vincent de Paul; and the very existence of Missions to the 'Heathen' implies that the soul of the Black is of equal value with that of the White. In the person of these Saints, the pagan renaissance met with its adequate rebuttal. I shall not, therefore, insert further comments between St. Camillus, and the next two Saints spoken of. After that, Europe will once more have tried to change its nature.

*

ST. FRANCIS XAVIER

1506–1552

G. K. CHESTERTON, when fifteen years old, won the Milton prize at St. Paul's with a poem on St. Francis Xavier: it was his literary début. His earliest critical biographer (1908) is said to have written: 'What G. K. C. made of that *singularly unpromising subject* I have forgotten, if I ever knew.' Doubtless he never knew. You do not *forget* Xavier. Relics of him are constantly even now being discovered in the East. Only some four years ago a huge cross with the medallion of 'Zaburio' upon it was erected at Yamaguchi in the west of Japan—paid for largely by non-Christians whose love and admiration for Xavier is still strong—and the opening ceremony was carried out by the non-Christian governor of the province.

Christ's Church is in essence Missionary. Christ was 'sent' by God to preach the Kingdom: in His turn He sent the Apostles: 'Go, teach all nations.' I spoke first about St. Paul; and ever since his day the world has been criss-crossed by the paths of men travelling to spread Christ's Faith. During the centuries I have spoken of, perhaps at first the great centres were Rome, and again that land, then the most scholarly of all, Ireland. Among the greatest missionaries of that time were the Benedictines. With the Middle Ages dawned the amazing missionary activity of the Franciscans and Dominicans. During the great religious revolutions of the sixteenth century, the Society of Jesus was founded, and St. Ignatius of Loyola, like St. Francis, wanted, at first, to spend his life converting Saracens. He had, however, to remain at home, and send others to that life of distant heroism that he would have loved to share. His intimate friend,

Francis Xavier, was not the first Jesuit to sail for missionary lands; but his name has eclipsed the others, and his memory is incomparably dear. Some of you may know *The Three Musketeers* and remember d'Artagnan; others, Cyrano de Bergerac. Romantic, audacious, unmoneyed gentlemen; dashing, gallant, poets despite themselves, never broken by the knocks of fate, proud, tender-hearted (even soft-hearted), full of charm—schoolboy heroes of romance and film. Xavier, had he somehow been de-sainted, could have been just that. As it is, he is real, and remains alive.

In the North of Spain, in a world scorched brown and grey, with dazzling torrent-beds and a sky blazing blue, was the frontier-fortress Xavier. A hollow square of terribly thick walls, with a tower in the middle. Winding passages within the walls, iron-clamped doors: a single loop-hole lit the chapel. Francis of Xavier and Jassu was born in that castle, April 7, 1506. His boyhood was austere and happy. He grew up, hard as nails, paramount in every sort of athletics, yet in love with songs; thick-haired; brown-faced; and a miracle of that personal magnetism that lasted him through life. But when he was six, disasters began. Spain was divided within itself; in 1512, war broke out; France and the Papacy were involved. Enough to say that part of the family of Francis went to one side, part to another; alone neutrality was impossible. One of his ancestral homes after another was destroyed; walls were demolished; lands confiscated; taxes imposed. The family was ruined but still fought. In 1520, the French and the men of Navarre were storming Pampluna and its handful of Castilians. Alone in the breach was standing Ignatius of Loyola. Up the slope dashed the attackers, two of Francis's brothers among them. He, only eleven, was left behind. A cannon-ball smashed Ignatius's leg, transformed his life, and led him at long last to found the Jesuits. Had Francis been but a few years older, it might have been he who brought Ignatius down.

Years went by: the Xavier family worked like beavers at a broken dam to restore their fortunes: Francis, the most brilliant, was sent to the World-University, Paris, and was extravagant. His mother, tormented, thought to bring him home. His sister, a Poor Clare nun, insisted that he must remain. He remained, but worked most of all at getting the Xavier titles to nobility re-recognised, and succeeded. Court, Cathedral, Commanderships-in-Chief—such were the visions that dazzled him. Yet—miracle of grace!—the worldly, brilliant, daring, above all fascinating lad remained clean. Never his the flabby lip, the sliding eye of lust; never his the collapse, nor the fever, nor the pestilence.

Francis went to Paris when he was nineteen. He was proud, but pride is not everything. Even the self-conscious 'gentleman' cannot always 'draw the line.' Francis then thought pride *was* enough: he accompanied his fellow-students—why, even his professor (who died of it)—on their expeditions, but refused to condescend. I think that the iron self-control of this passionate lad was running out when that young Swiss shepherd-genius, Peter Favre, began to share his lodgings. This exquisite character (no fool, I may say: he, too, was very 'tested') gave Francis pause. But the fastidious aristocrat, the intoxicating companion, the super-athelete, began to yield to a different temptation. Paris was then the home—when has it not been?—of new ideas. Through the black 'Gothic silhouette' of the old city, began to glitter the white marble and the gold of ancient, sceptical Athens. Francis nearly went 'unorthodox,' Modernist, we should say. Never lewd, he risked becoming intellectualist.

Just then, Ignatius of Loyola re-appeared. I might have liked to speak of him, but feeling him to be, as indeed he is, my spiritual Father, I have felt shy. Perhaps, someday, I may conquer that, and be allowed to do so. Well, there he was, a Spanish nobleman as truly as was Francis, but almost—as they say in S. Africa—'gone Kaffir,' He saw beyond money: beyond rank. Xavier hated and mocked him. Yet they met. And Ignatius conquered him. 'I have often heard our great Moulder of Men,' said Loyola's secretary afterwards, 'say that the stiffest clay he ever had to handle was Francis Xavier.' Who knows how, Ignatius made Francis see that money, titles, selfishness were as nothing compared to eternal issues—

to what one *was* (not what one had, not what one was named);
to what one might do for Others in the name of Christ—not
what one might do for Self, in the name of Self.

In 1533 Francis and Ignatius, with five others, promised
then to follow Christ in poverty and chastity, and after three
years (when their studies were finished) to start evangelising
the heathen. Ignatius was 43, Xavier, 28. They re-met at
Venice, 1537. For three years Francis trained himself to
serve. Above all, he worked in hospitals and prisons. Ordained priest, he fell sick and was given two months' life.
Ignatius told him to rest, and made him his secretary. Poor
Ignatius ! Someone complained that he could never get letters
to Rome answered. 'Whose fault is that ?' replied Ignatius,
smiling lovingly yet grimly. 'Señor Master Francis's. His
fingers are numb with cold, yet he will *not* realise that a fire
is meant to warm one's hands at.'

But into this sober, quiet, almost demure, existence a
bomb fell. In 1539 the King of Portugal asked Ignatius for
men to go as missioners to the Indies. Ignatius could offer
two. One got as far as Lisbon, one at the last hour fell victim
to sciatica. Ignatius, himself ill in bed, sent for Xavier.
'Francis,' he said, 'no one else can go—you must.' 'Certainly.'
said Xavier. 'At once; here I am ! *Pues, sus! heme aqui!*'
He had less than a day to prepare. He mended his own
cassock; Ignatius supplemented it by the gift of his own
waistcoat.

The journey to Portugal over the Alps was terrible. Snow-
drifts; torrents; precipices. Xavier, his muscles still true to him,
had to gallop after runaway horses, scramble down chasms,
manage the stables. A lad of the ambassador's retinue, who
hitherto had enjoyed life all too well over half Europe, fascinated by Francis, exclaimed: 'For the first time in my life have
I understood what it is to be a Christian.'

Lisbon was reached. On April 7, his thirty-sixth birthday,
thirty-five blunt-nosed transport-vessels, of which one in ten
used to founder, sailed for India, not reaching it till May of
next year, after a ghastly voyage. The emigrants were the very
scum of Portugal; Francis was for two months continuously

sea-sick; the very food, the very water, putrefied; Francis sacrificed all, his food, his clothes, his cabin, to the panic-stricken, cursing, murderous and promiscuous throng. They wintered at Mozambique, 'the Graveyard of Portugal'; and by then he was surrounded by an adoring troop of soldiers, sailors, slaves, and natives.

Impossible, I fear, even to suggest to you what his work became when he reached Goa. The Christianity of that commercialised, irresponsible world was too often but a farce. Officials were either worse corrupt than others or, having denounced abuses and been found out, were murdered. Francis cried in agony that Europeans were the worst enemies of themselves, of the natives, and of their Faith.

From 1542 to 1544, he made thirteen times—he, always sea-sick—the six hundred miles' journey to Cape Comorin, and back. He worked chiefly among the Paravar pearl-fisheries; organised a whole police as well as an education; was sent for by Rajahs to treat with brigands or pirates; in a world of dysentery, malaria, and elephantiasis, he made (and arranged for the solid instruction of) some thirty thousand converts by 1545. And be sure that his work has lasted ! Then came Ceylon; then sensuous Malacca, commercially undefeated as yet by Singapore. In that indolent air, he still slept in his palm-leaf hut, his head upon a stone. Thence to the 'Spice Islands,' west of New Guinea. He pursued the low Papuan type of natives into their mountains; the damp swarmed with insects and reeked with cloves. Head-hunters of Borneo; the cannibalism and hideous immoralities of Ceram—nothing quelled his hope. In the Moluccas, he found that it needed three years and nine months to get answers from Rome. Xavier, to whom every week of separation from his friends was anguish, cut out the very signatures of those letters and wore them next his heart, along with the copy of the vows he had made to Christ.

Yet these islands, always actively volcanic, with mud-fountains, explosions, and dust-clouds, and a brutalised population, were to him pure happiness. They should be called, he wrote: 'Islands of the Hope of God.'

Thrice shipwrecked, shaken to bits by travelling, often starving, attacked by Mohammedans, hiding in the bush. 'Never,' said he, 'have I been happier elsewhere, nor more continuously.'

Then he foresaw Japan. Remember, he was no fanatic, hurling himself unprepared into unknown lands. Before going there, he studied the language; studied, too, the Japanese religions; translated St. Matthew's Gospel into Japanese and learnt it by heart . . . how much more! Yet in Japan, more than anywhere, he seemed to fail—his whole life seemed to him *failure*: yet there more than anywhere he was, in fact, successful. He arrived after a real Gethsemani of *fear*: he was vibrantly sensitive; and his courage was true courage, just *because* he feared both what he foresaw, and, above all, the Unknown. He left but fifteen hundred to two thousand Christians behind him, seed, however, of an immense Church, often all but annihilated by persecution.

At last, in 1552, he left for China and arrived at San-Cian opposite the Si-kiang where Canton is. But no trading-vessel would take him to the land into which it was death for such as he to enter. Shivering-fits attacked him. 'Shall I reach China?' he wrote. 'I do not know. Everything is against it.' In November, alone with a Malabar servant and a Chinese boy he fell definitely sick. Bled and re-bled, he passed into delirium. In it he reverted to his childhood's language, Basque. The Name of Jesus was always on his lips.

We have full details of those last days. Imagine a mere frame-work of a hut, the palm-leaf thatch in fragments; the wind, setting the little lamp flaring and flickering; the ceaseless sound of waves; the Crucifix, fastened up by the Chinaman, with China invisible behind it, and the white face and shining eyes of Francis, who was all but speechless now, seeing nothing but the Crucifix, the memorial of Christ and of *His* death. Now were the maps rolled up; now was the travelling done with. Now was Ignatius, far away at his desk in Rome, now was even he bidden a last farewell. Now was the thrill of Paris, and now was the home in Spain—since which he had known *no* home—handed over to God, and left there. 'Into

Thy hands' I commend it all; my life and my eternity. The
night of December 2 passed by. Only the Chinaman watched
by the dying Saint. At 2 o'clock on the 3rd, when the winds
and the waters grew restless, Francis, too, stirred. The unmistakable and ultimate change touched him. The vigilant
native rose, put a lighted candle into the hand of Francis, and
held it there. Perhaps, in the breeze of the dawn, it expired.
But at that same hour, all alone, save for the Chinaman and
the companionship of Christ Crucified, Francis Xavier died.

If in the next-to-nothing I have said of this magnificent
man, this dearest of men, I can have conveyed to you some
millionth part of what he really was, how happy I should be.
Why, even I have seen how what he did has not vanished.
Once, down at Tilbury docks, during a Catholic procession a
devoted Goan had been impersonating Francis Xavier; and
at the end—imagine !—he threw his dress aside, ran, and
knelt to ask my blessing. It was because he had chanced to
be a seaman on a ship staffed by Goans, where I had said
midnight Christmas Mass for him and his compatriots. It was
the same Mass that four centuries ago, Francis Xavier had
taught his forefathers to venerate, to love, and never to forget.
I leave with you FRANCIS XAVIER, Christian, hero—to the end
I might say 'schoolboy,' despite the worn face and the thick
hair gone grey.

St. Francis Xavier, by Margaret Yeo (Sheed and Ward).

ST. CAMILLUS DE LELLIS

THE FIRST 'RED CROSS' MAN

1550–1614

THIS was the most extraordinary man. He had been the roughest of soldiers; had been reduced again and again to absolute destitution owing to his inveterate vice of gambling; he suffered from a horrible and seemingly incurable disease. Yet he altered in adult years the whole rhythm of his life; he lived to be old; and he became, and has remained ever since, the very Patron of the sick, of hospitals, and of the dying. And finally, he became literally (as has been with great insight noted and pointed out) the true founder of the Red Cross and originator of Field Ambulances. Hospitals originally were those parts of monasteries set aside for the care of the sick whether belonging to the monastery or coming from outside. But the origin of City Hospitals was almost entirely an affair of the thirteenth century, due to the work of Guy de Montpelier in France being taken up by Pope Innocent III, and centralised in the decrepit buildings set up by an Anglo-Saxon community in Rome. It was generalised all over Europe, though not least in Germany, in the shape of those Hospitals of the Holy Ghost, of which the Roman one is still, therefore, the universal Mother. I mention once more the names of St. Bartholomew's and St. Thomas's, which still exist; Bethlehem (Bedlam), which became an asylum; Christ's, which became a school.

All of these originated, or were developed enormously, about then. Do not imagine that even structurally these places are to be sneered at. Ventilation; sanitation; water-supply— all that was well understood. Do not dream that medical or surgical science was then at a low level. Indeed, they were far better than later on when much was forgotten and more destroyed. Operations on nerve and skull; the true origin of

76

venereal diseases; the use of red rays in cases of small-pox (with accurate statements of their results—knowledge which had to be rediscovered in the nineteenth century by the Danish Dr. Finsen, who gained the Nobel prize for doing so)—this and more was known, and used, in the thirteenth century and was largely forgotten two hundred and fifty years later. Historians relate the frightful degradation of hospital work. It was due both (as is usually asserted) to the destruction of religious orders devoted by tradition to such work, but also as I like to emphasise, to the revival (in the 'Renaissance') of the Greek worship of Nature, with its consequent horror of what was ill or ugly, and the shoving of such things out of sight. What is unseen soon sinks into forgetfulness. During the pagan renaissance, however, came, perhaps inevitably, the re-birth also of Christian Charity.

Camillus was born, in the Abruzzi, when his mother was sixty. In her intolerable anguish, she rushed to the stable and the child was born in the straw. His father had never been anything but a soldier—his life was a series of massacres and horror. He had grown rich on loot; but ended so poor that he had nothing to leave to his son save 'his dagger and his sword.' But by then Camillus was also a soldier, had gone crazy on gambling almost 'so soon as he could read,' had (when campaigning with his father against the Turk) fallen ill of the sickness from which the older man died, and returned suffering from a festering leg due to a 'slight scratch'—a wound never healed throughout his long life. In the hour of his bitter disillusionment, he saw two Capuchin friars, and vowed to reform himself. He broke his vow: twice more he made it, and twice more broke it. Now destitute, he entered a hospital, to be tended at the price of his own service. He was dismissed because of his violent temper, his eternal quarrels, his insane love for gambling—he slept with cards under his pillow and, for a game, would desert the sick. He re-became a soldier; was not at Lepanto only because he caught dysentery in Corfu; went through appalling campaigns against the Turks—the soldiery was reduced to such madness by starvation that they cut the very livers out of the dead and ate them. This Camillus never would do—*he* ate grass and horse-flesh. He joined a particular regiment simply because it had a reputation for gambling; he went to defend Tunis; returned; was discharged at Naples as for ever unfit for military service. Every item he still possessed, he staked; he lost the lot—already once, in Naples, he had staked his very shirt, and lost it. He became a beggar, to his scorching humiliation. But he was very tall, very strong, save for his rotten leg. They offered to make him bricklayer in a new Capuchin friary. He *had* to accept; but was so tormented lest this Franciscan environment should force him to keep his vow that he refused the very cloth the friars offered him to make a dress. He feared to commit himself to conversion. . . . But the frightful cold of winter drove him to give in. And in 1575, this more-than-Prodigal-Son, this man of wasted years and broken vows, did indeed give in.

He gave in; but not yet could he 'find his vocation.' He tried and tried again to enter a religious Order; but always the wound in his leg prevented him. His great succour was St. Philip Neri, in Rome, founder of the Oratorians, that affectionate, gay-hearted, yet most understanding man, who finally turned the sick soldier's ambitions towards serving, himself, the sick in hospitals, and so, towards the founding of that Congregation of Nursing Brothers which has perpetuated his name. In 1582 Camillus decided to group like-minded men around himself, and willed that they should wear on their shoulder a red Cross; and that in fact is the true origin of all later Red Cross movements. Useless to dwell on his early difficulties, among which was the sheer necessity of book-learning if he were to become a priest, which he now felt he ought to be. And it is pleasant to recall that his schooling, begun when he was thirty-two, ended happily and that he was ordained by an Englishman, Goldwell, bishop of a Welsh see, St. Asaph, and said his first Mass on the feast of the royal Scottish saint, St. Margaret.

The group developed rapidly and well; by 1588 Camillus started his first 'branch' at Naples, and he landed there fourteen years to the very day after he had been set on shore there, destitute, judged unfit for anything, and still a wastrel. Now I repeat, just when the pagan pomp of the Renaissance unfurled itself, care for human misery disappeared. When the beauty of the body was being worshipped, the very sight of sick or ugly bodies was abominated. The hospitals became such plague-spots of moral as well as physical horror that even had I space to describe them doubtless the B.B.C. would, rightly, forbid me to do so. The details given by contemporaries make it quite clear that they are not romancing. In the region of Rome alone, when pestilence swept it after the previous famine, sixty thousand persons died. It was in that year, and the next (1591), when Aloysius Gonzaga died owing to his work among the plague-stricken, that Camillus's work reached in some sense its apogee.

In winter, men were burying themselves in the very dung-heaps to keep warm; in the summer, the city was a mass of flies; the sick, for very lack of water, drank oil from the lamps, and worse; literally, Camillus would leave off work for but an hour or two in the night, to make mattresses that the sick should not lie in mud. In the early days of his conversion, he had twice seemed to hear our Lord call him, gently but very explicitly, a 'coward.' This had bitten deep. A physical coward, he very well knew he was not. As a soldier, he had been notorious for his reckless impetuosity; now fighting evil for Christ's sake, he remained always rather rough, and demanded much from his companions since it could not occur to him to demand but little from himself. Yet were his kindness, even his tenderness, extreme—it was a joy to watch him bathing and swaddling little babies, cooking small dishes for his convalescents; and his sheer intuition, spiritual sympathy, amounted to what was habitual second-sight. They could not tire of watching him bending over his sick folks, 'as though,' wrote one, 'he would communicate to them his very heart, his very soul.' 'I know not what more the most loving mother could have done for her sick child.' And no wonder, since nothing but the Spirit was carrying this man forward. For forty-six years he had had his wounded leg, which, as he aged, became excruciatingly painful; he suffered—you will not have to be too dainty if you would be realist—most terribly from stone; he had always to wear an iron truss; the soles of his feet were intolerable to walk on; for the last thirty months, everything he ate made him sick. He was so weak that he could hardly rise in the morning; yet, when he had visited five or six sick-beds, his heart had so rejoiced by reason of this serving of Christ, that his strength had returned.

Quite at the last, in a 'common infirmary,' he lay dying, and said the evening Angelus. An hour later, his infirmarian asked if he could not swallow something to refresh himself. 'Wait another quarter of an hour,' said Camillus, 'and I shall be refreshed.' After that quarter had passed, he stretched out his arms like a cross; said: 'Most Precious Blood,' as though the Red Cross and its Origin were still dominant in his mind; praised the Most Holy Name of God and died 'without a shudder, or change of his countenance,' which all the while had been cheerful and serene.

I would wish to end by making two points clear. First, Camillus is the true originator of the Red Cross, of Field Ambulances, of Advanced Dressing Stations, and of military hospitals. Camillus chose his red cross with the memory of the Crusaders in his mind; it became the badge of his men, of his Order, and of their work. Between 1595 and 1601, Pope Clement definitely sent the Red Cross Camillans to succour the wounded and dying on the actual field of battle; to ensure transport for bringing them back behind the lines; to prepare and manage hospitals on the way to the front; to provide stocks of medicinal and sanitary material. Dunant, who saw Solferino, and whose *Souvenir of Solferino* (1862) led up to the international agreement concerning the institution of ambulances everywhere, will have seen, at Solferino itself, the Red Cross of the Camillans at their work. Let us do homage to his book and its author; but let us not forget Camillus, his Brothers, and his Sisters, who anticipated that work in far less philanthropic days. And they did so—this is my second point—definitely for the love of Christ and because of His explicit command that we should tend the sick, and that if we do it not, we have left *Him* untended. In no other name or power did Camillus labour with unthinkable intensity for those forty years: himself in deadly pain; not ever seeking payment, or recognition, career or pension, but living also his personal life of prayer, and of penance; of poverty, of purity. I have experienced far, far too great kindness at the hands of doctors and of nurses in or out of hospital to think of those professions with anything but deep homage; but yet—different is the very glance, different is the touch, different the healing power and the interior communication of the soul, because of Christ, along with Him, and in His very person. This is Easter Sunday: our body shall sicken and shall die, nurse it as we will. But the soul survives; and by His power the very body shall arise, this time incorruptible, and we shall be 'man' complete, unsickening for ever.

See *The First Red Cross*, by Mrs. Oldmeadow (Burns, Oates and Washbourne); and *The Thirteenth, Greatest of Centuries*, by J. J. Walsh: Ch. XXI, and authorities there quoted.

Life of St. Camillus (Sheed & Ward).

ST. PETER CLAVER

APOSTLE OF THE NEGROES

1581–1654

WHEN speaking of St. Francis Xavier, I was so fascinated by the man as to say but little of his work, or rather, of the people he worked for. Peter Claver also was a missionary; but this time I shall want to say almost more about the mission than the man.

Never believe that the Saints are somehow born so, born the finished product, or at any rate doomed inevitably to become what they do become. How wavering and unsure were the beginnings of this man! Son of impoverished gentlefolk, he was sent for education to the Jesuit college at Barcelona. Like many an impressionable lad, he began to feel attracted to the sort of life his masters were leading: but he vacillated; whether to ask to join the Jesuits or not, he could not decide. Finally he did join them; and again hesitated—was he, after all, meant for something more aloof from external work? more of a monastery? He, like Xavier, met the right man at the right time—not, in this case, an overwhelming spiritual genius like Ignatius, but an old lay-brother Alonzo Rodriguez, porter in the College of Majorca whither Peter was sent for his philosophical studies. This old ex-business-man, whose wife and children all had died, had himself lost not one atom of his old power of shrewdly estimating character, nor any of his Spanish flame. He kept talking to the young student, whom his very studies intimidated, of the heroic life as spent in the far missions of the West Indies, and Peter Claver asked to be sent there. His request was granted, but he was told he had better be ordained before he went there. Frightened at the whole idea of the dedicated life, frightened—after embracing it—by the thought of vowing himself to it, disheartened by his very training once he had taken it up, he now shuddered at the irrevocablity of ordination. He left Seville, in 1610, not yet a priest. Even in America—his career was fluctuant, he ceased to want to be a priest and asked to become a lay-brother; but here, too, he met the necessary man—Fr. de Sandoval, an amazing character whose work lay entirely among the negro population there. Somehow companionship with Sandoval worked the miracle; Claver was ordained; and almost abruptly his heroic career, destined to last into his old age, began.

These negroes were slaves. The history of slavery as such has not always been so very terrible. That of the slave-*trade* always has. Or rather, it became so, the moment competition entered into it. England cannot be exempted from blame for these horrors. The moment cheap imported labour became desirable countries vied with one another to obtain the most lucrative contracts: the bodies of men became sources of revenue to would-be monopolists who bought cheap and sold dear. As from 1713, England was the chief holder. The time came when Newport in America was called 'another Liverpool': Bristol was no better: not till 1826 did the British colony of Jamaica permit free right to marry to those slaves of whom their masters spoke as 'black cattle,' asking whether an orang-outang were not a sufficiently good mate for a black woman.

In Claver's time, Portugal had the contracts. Slaves, victims at the outset of bloodshed and rape, were packed in bundles of six, necks and ankles chained together, wedged (wrote Sandoval) under decks where neither sun nor moon could penetrate, in a stench into which no white officer could put his head for fear of fainting. Maize and water was their food, once in twenty-four hours. About a third died on board; out of one cargo of five hundred, one hundred and twenty died in a night. A *duty* on such natives as died after landing was sheer incitement to kill off those who arrived living but *likely* to die. Yet so colossal were the profits, that even so it was worth keeping up the trade. Arrive they did, starving, covered with sores, more than half crazed, eating dirt to hasten their end, so frantically homesick were they; and turned out into a yard filled with such a reek that even the heroic Sandoval went into an icy sweat when a slave-ship was announced, remembering what he had been through last time. Among this it was that Claver laboured unceasingly for *thirty-eight years*.

When a ship was signalled, he went to the port, with medicines, disinfectants, lemons and brandy; he took always interpreters, needed indeed for men terrorised by having been told that their blood was to be used for dyeing the ship's sails, their fat for caulking its sides. He took them to their yards; washed them; dressed their wounds; made beds for them; downright mothered the maddened mob.

Now some colonial officer, listening, may exclaim: 'Ah! Another sentimentalising Missionary!' Forgive me, but— nonsense! Catholics are realists; so were Spaniards then; so was Claver. He exactly assessed the passionate love they felt for him: accurately he estimated their denseness, their glee; their prancings, their debauched or furious relapses; their ecstasies, their orgies. He could quell by sheer personality a whole mob running amok. To him men looked, not to scourge or gun, to put order into riot. And when, like him, you have again and again to rush to the air to be sick because of the stink, there is no room left for sentimentalism, especially if you know you must go back, and go on going back.

His work was not haphazard. With the physical healing went spiritual instruction always. And with what happened at Cartagena, his headquarters, went an endless following-up; untiring correspondence; regular tours of visits from village to village into which men had been sold, went an influence such that he could check, by a mere message, the flight of an entire population from a volcano—let them wait, he said, till he should arrive next day. Next day he came; led the negroes still quivering with panic, round the still-active crater, and planted a cross upon its lip. No one was injured. The hesitating youth had become the indomitable man, and walked serene along the very razor edge of peril.

At home, he concentrated upon two hospitals: St. Sebastian's, a general one; St. Lazarus, his favourite, restricted to lepers. True, he neglected no human item—lint, bandages, ointments, stuff for mosquito-curtains; saw to the lancing of sick men—nay, arranged concerts and so forth for them; but they—wise men—knew that this was but the almost negligible fringe of his mere *work*—as nothing compared with his *Self* or what stood as symbol of his Self—his mantle, just like those cloths and kerchiefs carried from the very body of St. Peter, in the *Acts*. That mantle served as robe for the leprous; veil for lupus-gnawed faces; pillow for the dying. 'Infectious'? Why, the very contact healed. The very edge of his cassock was ever in rags, so did they tear shreds from it: his very signatures were cut from certificates, the very hair that the barber had clipped from his head, the towels stained with the blood that doctors had drawn from him when he himself was sick, for all this people fought, so sure were they that he was what he was—a man filled full of GOD.

And with hospitals, went prisons. Constantly he was called to assist at executions. He wiped the criminal's wet forehead; he held him while the rope was being fitted to his neck. Once, if not oftener, it broke. Human Justice was inexorable. Claver held the shrieking man to his heart while a second rope was fitted. It, too, broke. A third rope made the poor victim die. But in a book left behind him in his cell, after a visit from Claver, the man had scrawled these words: 'This book still belongs to the happiest man in the world.' No wonder that the tale—be it historical, or, better than materially historical, a symbol—was broadcast, that a servant threw the water Claver had used for a baptism into a pan where some dead stalks were lying. Next day they had grown green and had re-flowered into life.

By 1650, Claver was old and broken. Year of torrential rains, and steaming heat. From Havana, plague reached Cartagena. The Jesuits flung themselves into this new service. Claver caught it; recovered; but found himself almost helpless. *Strapped to his horse*, he still insisted on visiting harbour, hospital, leper-house. Often he fainted as he went: at last he was shut up within a sick-room of his own. And (to our feeling) a tragic thing happened. Claver was left, in his last months, practically alone. Tragically, yet not inexplicably: the Jesuit community, doing double and triple duty (its ordinary

job, and its work among the plague-stricken, and work among
a population struck almost as fatally with panic), returned
home so exhausted that it could but fall into fitful sleep. But
'tragically,' not at all to Claver. This man (for, after all,
temperaments do not change) all his life, had really wanted
solitude, thought, prayer, but had been told by God that he must
serve, must do the maximum of exterior work. He loathed it
and loved it; was terrified of it but *did* it with a super-heroism.
This man, then, at the end, was *put* into a solitude. Assisted
only by one negro (who could not guess what a white man
might need, and *this* white man would never condescend to ask,
let alone complain) Claver lay there all day in the shattering
heat, the flies, amid the hateful scraps of food. In front of him
hung the picture of Alonzo Rodriguez, the Majorcan lay-
brother of—how many years ago Claver's life had been a unity.
He had willed to serve, for Christ's sake; and for Christ's sake
he had wholly served. When ships came to Cartagena, the
cannon thundered; tapestries were flung from balconies;
reviews glittered; officials galloped by. Had he ever noticed
them? Not he. In an interior solitude, but never loneliness,
had his life been spent—Christ, Souls, his Self. Solitude—not
non-human-ness. I tell you, he sickened of, he almost fainted
from, the horror of his task, but he *did it*.

In the mid-summer of 1654, the old man said that he was
dying. In an hour, the city knew it. Fr. Diego de Farina was
appointed Claver's 'successor.' Claver dragged himself to
his room and kissed his feet. On Saturday, September 5, he
was told that the City had decreed that the old Jesuit college,
his room included, must be demolished to make place for
better buildings. He said it did not matter (and even till Monday
he refused to receive the Last Sacraments). On the Monday,
the hammers of the workmen could be heard. He remained
serene. But, that night, they gave him the Last Sacraments
of the Church and he became unconscious. Again, in a
moment, the town knew of it. Even solitude was done with.

A throng besieged the college doors—officials, grandees,
laymen, priests. The Jesuits barred the gates. They were
burst in. One cry was heard: 'We wish to see the Saint!'

The passionate crowd would have stripped everything, so mad were they for relics. A friend could protect, alone, Claver's little picture of Alonzo, which in his unconsciousness he clung to. Then children filled the streets, refusing to move, calling for St. Peter Claver. Then came the negroes in a new army, breaking through even the children, and so into Claver's cell. Only after midnight, with unthinkable difficulty, was the house cleared, save for but a few. And between one and two o'clock of Tuesday, September 8, Feast of our Lady's Birth, St. Peter Claver died.

Do you want a hero ? Do you want a man co-crucified with Christ ? You have him. Peter Claver.

Captains of Christ, part III; by C. C. Martindale (Burns, Oates and Washbourne). *Aethiopum Servus*, by M. Petre.

ST. VINCENT DE PAUL

1580–1660

At the back of all modern philanthropy—work for children, the sick, prisoners—stands St. Vincent de Paul. He was living while Shakespeare lived: Milton outlived him. I could narrate the miserable history of France contemporary with him, but I need not. It was a land in which armies were sweeping to and fro, with their train of fire, murder, rape. A land where rapacious nobles intrigued against the king, and one another. A land where St. Francis de Sales and St. Jeanne de Chantal lived, and tried to do, but unsuccessfully, what Vincent succeeded in.

His parents were small farmers, in S. W. France. They kept no servant. Their son started as a shepherd. Intelligent, but visibly no use as a farmer, Vincent was put to school, his parents pinching to send him there. He became a 'private tutor' and a snob on the strength of it. He was ashamed of his shabby father, who limped. He studied in Spain, then for seven years at Toulouse; he was ordained and hoped for a bishopric from his patrons. Then, returning home by sea, he was captured by Turkish pirates and taken to Tunis.

Here, having (like other slaves) been paraded round the town, thumped in the ribs, examined as to teeth, made to run and wrestle, he was sold first to a fisherman and then to an aged alchemist, man of Science in those days. This man, sent for by the Sultan, and dying of home-sickness on the way, bequeathed Vincent to a nephew, who re-sold him to an apostate Christian from Nice. One of this man's three wives was touched by Vincent's piety, and in the long run they all escaped to France. Here a Cardinal Vice-Legate, Montorio, took a fancy to Vincent—partly because of the queer arts he had learnt in Africa; he was a ventriloquist and could make a skull 'talk'—and finally took him to Rome, and in 1609 sent him home on a diplomatic mission to Henry IV of France, who was trying to unite all Europe against Austria and Spain. What this mission was Vincent never revealed; and such was the change in him, that he sought no personal remuneration or recognition from it.

He lived, at first, in extreme poverty in Paris; he was appointed almoner by the ex-queen Margaret de Valois; he met and lived with M. de Bérulle, the Oratorian; he was made parish-priest of the destitute parish called Clichy. He therefore learnt by experience what royalty, what Paris, what the fields, what life in community, were; and abruptly, he was sent to be tutor to the 'young devils' (as their aunt described them), sons of the overwhelming nobleman, Philippe Emmanuel de Gondi, Comte de Joigny, General of the Galleys.

In that palace, Vincent lived as austerely as a monk. He ended by dominating, if not the children, at least their parents. He persuaded—a true miracle—the Lord to renounce a duel; the Lady, to visit the sick. Appalled at becoming a 'personage,' Vincent literally fled to a very modest parish: here, during the plague, he made some astonishing conversions among nobles, and perceived that—such was their generosity—charity needed some organisation. He wrote a simple Rule; and this, 1617, is the true origin of the Sisters of Charity and of much besides. A Community of Priests was foreseen, who should work in villages, seek no preferment, and live from a common purse. But the Gondis insisted that Vincent should come back and live with them. However, almost at once, Mme. de Gondi died; and the Count became—can you credit it ?—himself an Oratorian. Vincent was free to begin his life's work; but he was fifty years old !

I have to leave to one side an extraordinary episode. Gondi had been General of Galleys, which were manned by criminals chained to their thwarts and stripped to the waist in order to be flogged. Such vessels, in warfare, caught fire, blew up, or were sunk. They were a hell. Vincent, who had become intimate with the filth, reek and wickedness of Paris prisons, equipped a hospital whither the most infectious diseases might be carried, and was appointed chaplain-general to the galleys in 1619. Did he learn his business from within, by himself becoming for a while a galley-slave? It is not certain; but I think he did. I now mention a few of the other things he did, disregarding mere dates. He was sure that the formation of priests was essential. I think that the country clergy of France had simply despaired. The peasantry were 'black animals' who lived by grubbing or roots, while armies swept to and fro, and a few great lords lived in crass luxury. The dumb misery of the countryside at the one end; pulpit 'oratory' and tyranny at the other. Vincent created his Lazarists, priests so called because at first they lived in a monastery dedicated to St. Lazarus. Then he remembered towns. He felt he had deserted the thousands of miserable paupers within the walls of cities. Then he remembered his own enslavement in Tunis —at least forty thousand Christian slaves existed in N. Africa —some of them, little English boys, carried off by pirates. Not till 1830 did Algerian pirates cease from off the seas, nor the African sun and African vice cease to tempt Europeans to crime and to apostasy. Then his priests began to go north- wards—to Ireland: Cashel and Limerick. To Scotland, and the Hebrides. Then to Poland; then to the 'White Man's Grave,' Madagascar. Egypt, Brazil, China beckoned to him. To-day it is China that most of all sees his Lazarists at work.

But in the Catholic Church there is no such thing as priest *versus* laity. He resolved to animate the laity too with the will to serve for Christ's sake. Women, who had wished to dedicate their lives to God, had been forced, by tradition and popular opinion, to do so within closed convents. Vincent brought them out of their enclosure, and created both those Sisters of Charity (whose wide white caps are bound to be familiar to all of you who know the world at all), and those 'Ladies of Charity' who, without becoming Sisters, devote their lives so far as possible to the service of the needy.

Vincent found that by 1650 there were forty thousand completely destitute persons in Paris out of a population of five hundred thousand. Four out of every fifty persons were completely destitute. He began with the children, whom their

frantic parents cast out into institutions of which it is not too
much to say that they became the homes of dreadful cruelty,
if not wholesale massacre. He, in his land, was the first to look
after little children. And he knew each baby by its name. In
those days, when to venture alone outside the house was ruin
to reputation, he told his nuns that they must know no convent
but the sick-room, no cloister but the street. And—would
you believe it?—Court-ladies, who, appalled by the insincerity,
the sham, of fashionable life, would else have buried themselves in cells, no less than the heavier-witted women of the rich
but inelegant classes, flocked to his call. I have no room to
speak of his work for the insane: his house at St. Lazare
(of which you may know the name because of a big Paris
station that still bears it) was filled with those who were only
not mentally but morally defective.

Nor have I room to speak of his connection with the
secular, political, and royal history of France. He hated those
duties: still, when Louis XIII required to die in Vincent's
arms, the Saint was there. Enough to say that even during the
ghastly siege of Paris, in the very Court there existed his group
of devoted women, working for the relief of those whom the
Court considered rebels. Ladies lavished their jewels upon his
work; tradesmen poured out their wares gratis upon him.
But by now he was very old, and very tired. Sleepiness invaded
him—he said that the brother was ahead of the sister—sleep
had anticipated death. His legs swelled; he sat all day in an
armchair at his enormous correspondence. Then they grew
ulcerated; he was nailed to his bed, and could raise himself
only by a cord from a hook in the ceiling. All his old friends
and associates were dying; he knew that he, too, would very
soon follow them; but never did the smile fade from his clean-
cut lips, nor his mind (as his letters prove) waver. They
whispered sentences from the Scriptures to him: he loved to
answer 'Paratum !' ('Ready'). (I have asked myself whether
Thackeray, when he wrote Colonel Newcome's 'Adsum,'
'Here, sir !' had been reading of St. Vincent.) Finally he said:
'I believe,' and then, 'I trust,' and at four in the morning of
September 27, 1660, seated in his armchair, he died, perfectly

serene, at the precise hour at which for so many years, he had risen to pray.

Vincent began, if you remember, with the qualities of a peasant rather ashamed of his estate and determined to better himself. Not *perfectly* scrupulous about money; looking forward to rank—even ecclesiastical; showing unmistakable signs of what he himself called his 'dried up, caustic temper,' and victim of 'black and boiling moods.' I think it was his experience of slavery that supplied his drastic lessoning—that turned him into a man utterly detached from money, undazzled by even royal rank; and won somehow for him by a kind of universal instinct the title of 'le bon M. Vincent'—untranslatable word, not merely 'good,' but implying a lovableness in the goodness—no condescension in the kindness—almost, our *dear* St. Vincent. But in that kindness was no softness: his innumerable letters are shrewd, vivacious, affectionate, but most uncompromising: from those who proposed to join him and to work with him, he demanded *all*. Alas! it is so easy to serve Christ by fits and starts, when in the mood, in some ways only, with reserves.

Once more, the secret of the Saints is, that they judge life and work upon the scale of Christ. Christ *never* deserts; gives Himself no holidays; keeps nothing back at all. Hence, maybe, Vincent's courage. His portraits show him with almost clumsy features, yet with eyes as wistful as they are humorous, and you would probably not guess from them his ardour, indeed, his audacities. Yet this man, willing to wait so very very long for the time *really* to work, was wanting to sanctify *all* priests; serve all hospitals and prisons; save all little children—and so, by uncloistering his nuns, he has indeed come to stand at the back of those millions of devoted women who all over the world and ever since have been doing their part of the work that was and is so needed; and it is hardly too much to say that this is the man who is inspirer of all such women's work in our modern world; and it was his name that was so spontaneously and immediately chosen by Ozanam, whom I hope to mention on May 1, when he, in his turn, inaugurated those Conferences which set laymen everywhere at the service of the disinherited by life; and for me it is really like going home when, from time to time, I visit that great Vincentian house that stands on the steep slopes and beneath the smoky skies of Sheffield.

The Heroic Life of St. Vincent de Paul: Henri Lavedan (Sheed and Ward). The standard edition of St. Vincent's letters was published in Paris, 8 vols., 1920–1923.

The glories of the Renaissance lasted for but a brief space; the miseries for which it was responsible endured, and are still bearing their pitiable fruits. For, the worship of Power, of Wealth, and of the Flesh, expressing itself in absolute monarchies that sought to play Cæsar over the Church itself, and in the insane extravagance of Courts and the vast fortunes of a few men only, and a blatant immorality, disgusted those who took the trouble to think, and drove the mass of men to desperation. But the very men who, by reason of their superior positions, and intelligence, might have helped, really hindered advance; for their disgust displayed itself in cynicism, and cynicism never assists anything. They profited by the system that they sneered at while they could, knowing very well that it was doomed.

The French Revolution then broke out, and a dozen other revolutions followed it; and on the top of all this came Napoleon before Europe had had time so much as to draw breath.

Flimsy philosophies were followed by the rapid advance of science in the material sense; and a jungle-growth of theory which confused men's minds worse than ever. It was in this most unpleasant period that the next Saint we speak of, lived. To my mind, his life, and the Apparitions of Lourdes and the subsequent history of that shrine, are a kind of spiritual, and sufficient, rebuttal of the ugly materialism of the time.

*

ST. JOHN BAPTIST VIANNEY: THE CURÉ D'ARS

WHAT BEING A PRIEST MEANS

1786–1859

THIS will be, perhaps, the most paradoxical of the Saints of whom I am speaking, simply because you cannot detect any natural reason for things turning out as they did. John Baptist was the fourth son of some peasant-farmers in the village of Dardilly, north of Lyons. The French peasantry is above all realist. It sees, understands, and uses the earth; manages its animals; develops its families. When it possesses the Faith, it regards its doctrines as just as solid as anything else. At any rate, this was true until one revolution after another set the world rocking round it; until all sorts of experiments in atheist education and then the cheap press, and finally the cinema, completed its confusion. The Great Revolution (1789) soon closed the churches, silenced the bells, proscribed priests, and guillotined them when it caught them. God, as Comte was to say, had been escorted to the frontier, without even those thanks for interim-services rendered that the philosopher was prepared to offer Him. Secretly, now and again, Mass was said in barns; behind rocks; but not till he was ten could John make his First Communion. In 1800 the churches were re-opened. God always returns.

The lad had grown up pious, but very dull. A clumsy, raw-boned ploughboy. Yet at nineteen he got leave to live with an admirable man, the Abbé Balley, to be educated for the priesthood. It seemed that nothing could be driven into that thick skull. It was now that he began to pray hard, and to fast. Both these practices cleanse the soul's eye, and have, therefore, their effect even on the intelligence.

Napoleon was throwing France and all Europe into new confusion; in 1809 Vianney was called up, started, fell ill, went to hospital, failed to catch up with his regiment, and in sheer exhaustion, technically deserted. A magistrate, out-of-love with the imperial regime, sheltered the lad, who did jobs about the house. Finally, his parents exchanged him for a younger brother. He entered a seminary, hoping to prepare for the priesthood. Very slow of intellect, he could learn neither Latin nor moral theology; they plucked him in his exams; they sent him away. At long last, M. Balley pushed him through; he was ordained, just two months after Waterloo, for some poor country parish where they wouldn't need a wiseacre. For three years he acted as curate to M. Balley, and at once what I must call the *instinct* whereby man recognises Sanctity, displayed itself. Everyone wanted to hear the terrified lad preach; and to go to him for confession, though for a very long time he was not so much as allowed to hear confessions. At thirty-two he was appointed parish priest to the village of Ars, sleepy hollow in the dullest of districts, yet which, said he, in sudden prophecy, would not be able to hold all these who should some day come to it.

The backwash of any period of tumult is apathy. His parishioners, deprived for so long of priests, were crassly ignorant; they compensated for the hard work of the fields with heavy drinking (not a French vice), blasphemy (a vulgar trick, that may mean next to nothing), and a mania for dancing that too often ended disastrously. Everyone was friendly to their new pastor; no one expected anything special from him. Yet they received it. He appeared in the pulpit—big round forehead, hollow cheeks, fiery blue eyes that looked right into you, a smile like a child's, and bony, praying hands. He laboriously learnt his sermons: yet he recited no phrase of them. Eloquence has been defined as 'saying things to people.' All that he said was *said;* all of it was 'thing'; all of it reached a *person.* The result is, that while no end of fragments of his sermons could be quoted, not one of them is anything but a platitude. 'My God, you see how I love you; but I do not love you enough. We shall see God—have you ever thought of that? We shall see Him—we shall see Him.' Yet platitudes are the profoundest things in the world; we are so accustomed to them that we see nothing 'in' them—their truths are like the unnoticed air we breathe. But Vianney saw *in* them their truth to its very depths: all that he said meant an infinity to him; never a formula—never a *cliché*—he meant the whole maximum of what his words could mean, and not a soul doubted it, and all responded.

Having perceived that to be a priest means to sacrifice your whole life for others for Christ's sake, he *acted* on this. He was the perfect realist; literalist. Bit by bit his furniture disappeared: he slept on two planks; he cooked enough potatoes for a week, and ate a couple at midday and in the evening; sometimes an egg; sometimes a cake of black corn. Do not exclaim: 'How criminal not to take better care of yourself'— he lived to be seventy-three, working all day long. What 'all day long' meant, you shall hear in a minute. After ten years, the village and its district had changed so much that M. Vianney could exclaim: 'Ars is no longer Ars !' And it was much happier. Why, automatically, the farm-labourers were decently looked after, and allowed due rest. You may not guess the slavery possible in a lost countryside: as tragic as it is grotesque when the country apes the town—believes, poor land, that towns are worth imitating ! I beg you to recall that this transformation was not easy. Men, whom it paid to have other men get drunk in their cabarets; lads, furious that their girls resisted them; girls, who could no more make their living off their bodies, attacked Vianney in scurrilous ways; and in his own self, he had the intolerable monotony of the Fight versus Self to endure. Yet the conquest came.

He began to be known; to be invited. Everyone was stupefied. When he said what had a thousand times grown stale, behold it was alive, aflame, a thunderbolt. And in the confessional, it was clear that he quite simply *read souls*. Not only he knew what a man meant when he spoke, but he knew (even in exact detail) what he had left unsaid. But don't picture a sort of mystical ecstatic. Vianney was shrewd with all a peasant's shrewdness; he stood no nonsense; he even rose to epigram: 'It is a pity,' he said to a casual huntsman with his dog and gun, 'that your soul is not as beautiful as your dog.'

The man stood, at first, petrified; cleaned up his conscience; was told he was called to be a Trappist—and became one.

The unbelievable happened. Without one word of advertisement, no publicity, no press paragraphs, no stunt-ism, the world began to know of M. Vianney. France flocked to Ars; men came from other lands, from overseas. Coach-services were organised, special trains were run; homes became lodging-houses; inns, hotels. And this was his day's history: At one, he rose. He prayed solitary in the church, and then heard confessions of women till six. Then he said Mass, and was at the general disposition till eight. Then he went to a 'providence' home he had organised, and had half a glass of milk. At eight-thirty he heard confessions of men till eleven, when he taught the children. At noon, taking a quarter of an hour to cross the crowded, seething square, he went to eat (standing), his potato or two, thronged by questioners. At twelve-thirty he visited the sick, always surrounded, as he moved, with visitors; then till five, he heard confessions of more women; and till eight, of men. He then held his evening service and preached; he prayed, heard more confessions, and went to bed at midnight. And up at one. And this, for thirty years. And this, while my own grandfather was alive.

Naturally the criticism lavished upon him—even from his fellow-clergy, when they were conventionalists—was vitriolic. And the almost terribly wonderful thing about it is, that in his humility he agreed with all of it. The one thing that this man, who was almost crushed to death by the throngs of a hundred thousand, had desired was solitude. What he was sure he could not do was to direct souls. When he was fifty-nine, realising that in any case his work was beyond him, he asked for a curate. They sent him an exceedingly conceited and 'managing' gentleman who, after eight years of real, though unconscious, persecution of M. Vianney had, under pressure of popular opinion, to suggest his own removal. Yet Vianney was so sure of his own incompetence that more than once he actually tried to *run away*. Back he had to come. They made him a Canon. The Marquis de Castellane obtained that the Minister of Public Instruction should recommend him to the Emperor

The Curé d'Ars fulfilled his life just in being a perfect priest. Saint John Bosco was also a priest, but expressed himself in terms of what certainly preoccupies our modern world—the social problem: philanthropy and education. The difference between him and the 'naturalistic' social worker, or philanthropist, or educator, lies in the fact, precisely, that he built wholly upon a supernatural foundation. Hence his achievement was different. His influence was far deeper; his work both wider and more permanent; its total results issued into something immeasurably higher, purer and more spiritual than did the work of men who either excluded God from their calculations and endeavours, or were unable to reach, rely on, and (dare I say) utilise Him, as Don Bosco did.

We can very easily observe, in our own time, the diverging methods—the Christian and Catholic one; and the 'secular' one. By studying men like Don Bosco we ought to be able to see not only that, but why the secularised method always turns out badly. 'Quem Deus vult perdere'—I have been tempted to think that governments, when they try so desperately hard to secularise politics, education, social reform, and the rest, are being all but driven by God to engineer their own disaster, that they may realise the facts, and learn better, or that at least their successors may do so. But no; God drives no man to such insanity or to such suicide. Yet if men *will* not learn, nobody can force them to: in so far as the Agnostic State survives and operates, let alone the anti-God State-school, the catastrophe will inevitably follow, and we shall see more graft, more grab, more war, more disintegration.

*

SAINT JOHN BOSCO

1815–1888

JOHN BOSCO was born of very poor parents, in a tiny village near Turin. One hundred thousand persons came to his funeral. How was this ?

Piedmont is a land of ancient history, wide plains gorgeous with vine and maize, and braced by keen breezes down from the Alps; its people are tough, genial, ambitious hard-working. John's father, a small jobber, died all too soon, leaving his valiant wife to care for her stepson, Antonio, and her own two sons, Giovanni and Giuseppe. She brought them up rigorously and lovingly in the poor cottage; the small John, walking four times a day to school, covered thus twelve miles daily. Her stepson began to grow up a bully, and jealous of his half-brothers. He became better later on, but at first made life frankly miserable for his step-mother and half-brothers.

John, who had an astounding faculty for *dreaming*, decided at *nine*, on the strength of a dream in which he saw himself changing children from beasts into lambs, to become a priest and devote his life to *children*, and began at once. He haunted every caravan and fair; learnt to walk tight-ropes, to become acrobat and conjuror at cost of often-broken nose. . . . and provided fascinating entertainments, which he wound up with the rosary and a sermon. . . . Then this round-headed boy with tousled hair took to his books; he simply could not forget; between a Christmas and an Easter he learnt the whole Latin grammar.

But Anthony was making life intolerable. His mother sent John away to work, and to learn. One experience he retained and used. The priests managing his elementary school were correct, aloof, chill. Bosco's temperament would never have allowed him to become that; but here he learnt he *ought* not to become it. Nor ever did he. Yet, though he ate but maize and chestnuts, worked all day as house-boy and billiard-marker; began to exercise his magnetism and became the centre of a group; beat professional athletes and acrobats at their best performances; worked late into night with one tallow dip, it looked as if he had no future. He had to drop his studies, being too poor. Suddenly, all went right. Charity succoured him; he won prizes. At twenty he entered the seminary at Chieri; after six years' study he was ordained. He had retained his irrepressible gaiety, despite his stiff, semi-Jansenised professors.

While finishing his training in another college he studied the Turin slums. Their degradation was then appalling. He could achieve no contact till one day a sacristan smacked the head of a big oaf who stood staring and had answered that he didn't know how to serve the Mass John was about to offer. 'I won't have my friends treated like that,' exclaimed the priest. 'Your *friend?*' 'The moment anyone is ill-used he becomes my friend.' The lad was brought back; next Sunday he fetched others; in but a few months over a hundred were arriving. For three years this uproarious horde had for playground the courtyard of the college.

I wish I could mention the names of those who helped Don Bosco. Saints are among them. But in a quarter of an hour, impossible. Indeed, he soon met obstacles. An old priest put a thistle-grown field at his disposal—but the priest's housekeeper wouldn't have the noise, and she got the leave withdrawn. He obtained a chapel near some mills; the millers and their men said the lads were ruffians (so they were, half of them) and got *that* leave withdrawn. The clergy themselves objected to boys from their parishes hanging around Don Bosco. The Marquis of Cavour (father of the statesman) was told that Bosco was organising a political conspiracy, and he was watched by the police. But it was the police who were converted, not Bosco arrested. When he visualised and announced what the future held they said he was a megalomaniac: two priests were sent to—literally—'take him for a ride.' A drive to the asylum. Bosco guessed their errand, followed them to the carriage, and 'After you,' said he politely. They entered. Bosco slammed the door and called out: 'To the asylum.' Off the driver went, and took quite some time to get the poor men out. . . . Italians have a caustic sense of humour. Bosco had scored. After some setbacks he established himself, in 1846, in a slum-centre, obtained his mother's companionship, and started what he called his oratory, a group of four hundred lads of the roughest. Hitherto all this had been in the margin of his regular work; now he could devote himself to his true apostolate.

I cannot even outline his life, which was adventurous enough: Italy was in the throes of every sort of political and social upheaval; extreme disorder often prevailed. Half a dozen times Don Bosco was murderously set upon. Once a man shot at him through the window as he sat teaching. The bullet passed under his arm, ripping the cloth. 'A pity,' said he; 'it is my best cassock.' And he continued the lesson. More than once his terrific straight left sent the would-be garrotter flying; and a fascinating episode is that of the enormous dog Grigio, many-times-over-mongrel, who appeared intermittently from nowhere, refused a kennel, ate who knows how, hurled himself upon assailants, escorted the priest through dangerous patches, and once snarlingly refused so much as to allow him to go out. Had he done so, he would have fallen straight into an ambush.

Willingly I leave to one side his associations with great personages; enough to say that the most anticlerical officials were won by his frankness and forthrightness, and that twice when he was in Paris, Victor Hugo came, Nicodemus-like, by night, and made to him a profession of faith that his melodramatic will does not disannul. . . . I must concentrate on his educational work, and on his personality, and even these I must interweave. He began by realising that to-day every religious enterprise on behalf of the young must have its educational aspect, just as no educational enterprise is of the slightest lasting value without being firmly based upon religion. The latter fact is proved by the whole of the last hundred and fifty years of European and American history; and experience forces the former one upon us. His groups of boys then at once included classes; the classes became schools—very simple schools developed others—others of a much higher grade. But to me his agricultural and professional schools have always been the most interesting: Italy and Spain herein may have more reason to be grateful to Bosco than to almost anyone else at any time, save perhaps the Spanish Jesuits.

His miraculous influence over the young enabled him definitely to exchange the almost prison-like existence in the schools of his day for something far more human. He gave liberty without loss of discipline; he was gentle without any softness; endlessly understanding without complaisancy; he shared in, and indeed initiated every sport, yet never lost his dignity. From Pope and prince down to gutter-snipe, he used the same free, dry, gay repartee. Only once, that I can remember, was he caught out. 'What,' said he to a rather talkative young ruffian, 'is the most remarkable thing you've seen?' 'Don Bosco.' . . . The patron of all hikers, he was the first, maybe, in modern Europe to understand the virtues of sheer noise. But he made it musical. . . . Not even—well—the brass band of Rhodesian Chishawasha, shattering the silence of the veld, has so enchanted me as have the Salesian brass bands under the suave skies of Italy. 'Salesian'? Bosco soon saw he must create an 'Order' of men to support him. That Order, characteristically named after the witty, gentle, vigorous St. Francis de Sales, consists to-day of some nine thousand men. In Italy alone it has a hundred and fifty houses; in the rest of Europe about a hundred and seventy; in America two hundred and forty; in Asia, Africa, Australia about seventy. These enterprises range from seminaries and parishes, through colleges, all sorts of schools, but especially industrial and professional, to hostels, emigrant-institutions, and hospitals or leper-colonies. Parallel to this he founded the women's society of our Lady Help of Christians, with about six hundred houses, whose work again covers the whole civilisational and religious ground, from kindergartens through municipal schools to schools for domestic economy and the like.

Towards the end of his life Don Bosco developed two special interests: one was England, whither the Salesians came in 1887; there are thirteen of his houses now within the Empire, the latest opened being near Macclesfield, a training college for foreign missionaries especially for India, Siam, and Palestine. And these Missions quite haunted his mind towards the last. Already in 1856 he had begun to think of England; in 1875 he sent his first missionary band to South America: Patagonia, Tierra del Fuego, the Isles of Magellan, then Ecuador; deep into Brazil, Paraguay, Bolivia. . . . I will not attempt to catalogue his missions to-day, the Salesians work all the world over.

Yet what, indeed, is all this exterior work, let alone the homage that surrounded his last years? When he was at Lyons the business of driving him through the crowds was such that the poor cabman lost his temper and cried out: 'I had rather drag the devil than drive a Saint.' And in Paris the church of our Lady of Victories was crammed two hours before he came to say Mass in that 'refuge for sinners,' and a poor woman exclaimed to a questioner: 'You see, it is the Mass for sinners, and it is to be offered by a Saint. . . .' But what is all this, compared to, precisely, the man's sanctity? In a way Bosco lived simultaneously in four worlds—that exterior one, symbolisable by the absolute *town* that the Turin Oratory and its appurtenances are the world of dreams—and believe me, an exact scientific study of his recorded dreams would be of infinitely more value to psychologists than that of diseased mentalities˙in Viennese hospitals; the world of souls, into which he read with an accuracy far beyond telepathy or second sight (whatever these may mean); and the world of God.

His purity, perfect to the very roots of his thought, enabled him, as our Lord promised, to 'see God,' and therefore, perhaps, to read so clearly within his fellow-man; his total trust was such that literally he built up his entire work out of nothing; his lovable sarcasms that never hurt; his transparent simplicity; his bluff gaiety, despite terrific work (from youth he had promised never to sleep for more than five hours) and great physical pain and complete self-denial—all this was an affair not of temperament, not of talent merely, but from God. 'God,' says the Introit of the Mass said in his honour on April 26th, 'gave him wisdom and very great prudence, and a *breadth of heart* wide as the sea-sands.' And later on: 'He believed, hoping against hope, so that he became father of many peoples, as was said to him.' And read its epistle, taken from St. Paul's letter to the Philippians, iv, 4–7; it is, so to say, the essence of Don Bosco. Great men and their work cannot just be imitated. May God give to his successors a double portion of his spirit. I have, indeed, encountered that spirit, alike in his houses beneath the burning sky of Cape Town, and in the playgrounds more grim, but no less gay, of Battersea.

The Christian can never be a pessimist. He believes in the 'Holy Ghost: the Holy Catholic Church.' The Church can never cease to exist; and in her is the very source of Sanctity, that can never be dried up. For, being the Body of Christ, she lives by His imperishable life; she breathes by His Spirit.

Hence we regard it as morally certain that Saints are existing to-day quite as much as ever they did; that they are already the salt of the earth—the ever-new lights that are yet to be set upon their lamp-stands. Hence, when speaking of 'Saints without the St.' we do not mean to anticipate the decision of that authority which alone has the right to proclaim, officially, to the world that a Saint has lived among men, but merely to witness to the sure and certain fact that the Christian Life *is* heroically lived and, so far as the average eye can see, has been heroically lived in the case of this man or of that. I do not know that any one of the men whose names will now be quoted, will ever be 'canonised,' nor indeed that they were worthy of canonisation. Not all the 'canonisable' are canonised! But at least we can gratefully affirm that from these men the average plodding, apt-to-be-disheartened Christian can draw profound encouragement and inspiration; that he can see in them greatness, Catholic greatness; nay, can derive from them that refreshment that contact with holiness always affords: anything further he leaves to time and to God.

✻

SAINTS WITHOUT THE 'ST.'

How can I get across to you, to-night, what I want ? I cannot call the men I shall speak of 'Saints,' for they have not been canonised, and I cannot anticipate the verdict of the Holy See. And I can hardly, in one talk, provide even miniatures of them—hardly thumb-nail sketches.

Well, take Frédéric Ozanam, born 1813, who died in 1852. He lived in France during a disgusting period of the most flimsy forms of scepticism and unreal, affected religionism. He was an obstinate, lazy, passionate, disobedient boy; then, abruptly, 'good' as from his first Communion; then fiercely attacked by doubt—Frenchmen do get these fierce attacks, and catch fire over theories, we, vaguely yet conventionally educated, as a rule, just slop into 'nothing-in-particular-ism.' At eighteen he went to Paris for Law. Among his fellow-students he found only three who would so much as call themselves Christians. His loneliness would have been awful, had he not met and been housed by that great scientist and great Christian, Ampère. There he saw all the best men of science of the day. His own scientific, literary, and professional progress led him from one triumph to another: Doctor of Law, Doctor of Letters, Professor of Commercial Law at Lyons, nominated by Cousin himself for a professorship in Paris (Foreign Literature), and finally held a Chair for life in the Sorbonne. If he has not covered his name with international and enduring glory it may be because he was too all-round brilliant; but even more, I think, because of the other side of, or rather the soul of, his life.

I omit, then, the ardent intellectual defence of Christianity that within the university—and as a journalist, and along with men like Bailly, Montalembert, Lacordaire—he provided and recall that his father was a doctor who (it was found after his death) had rendered one-third of his service gratis to the poor. As a lad of but twenty, Ozanam founded the St.

Vincent de Paul societies which exist to-day all over the globe, to which no imaginable work of personal charity is alien, but which, above all, visit the poor in their own homes. They number to-day 154,955 active members; and 78,620 honorary members (1930). Essentially a lay work, may it also be a *young* work; hardly anything can so well uproot the young from their intolerance, their conventionality (and our cult of unconventionality is just as conventional as anything can be, not least to-day when the alleged 'revolt' of youth follows all the rules so accurately), and from their ignorance of the *great* sufferings, *great* injustices, great heroisms of life.

Radiantly happy as husband and as father, Ozanam, no more than thirty-nine, was dying. On August 15th, supported by his wife, he went for the last time to Mass, and the priest, who was dying too, insisted that none should have the privilege of administering Holy Communion to Ozanam save himself. That was the last Mass that this priest and that Ozanam offered to God. On September 8th, home in Marseilles, he died. All over the Catholic world his work is now taken for granted.*

In the same church where Ozanam had been baptised Contardo Ferrini was baptised in 1859, forty-six years later. At twenty he took his law-degree with honours higher than any ever granted to such a student at Pavia. He did post-graduate work at Berlin on the very morrow of the Kulturkampf; and returned to the Universities of Italy as professor of Roman Law in the Universities of Messina, Modena, and again Pavia. His expert knowledge of Byzantine and of Roman Penal Law was such that the great German historian, Mommsen, is said to have cried out that in Ferrini's person the primacy in this branch of erudition had passed from Germany to Italy.

Yet I mention this only that you may see how thoroughly he was involved in all the scepticisms, all the social upheavals,

*Et que les catholiques de France, qui m'ecoutent, sachent que l'Angleterre leur est reconnaissante; et que le monde entier salue, en Ozanam, la charité Française, qui n'est si sublime, si universelle, que parce qu'elle est catholique !

as well as in all the erudition, of the day. His temperament was fiery in the extreme; he was devoted, like the present Sovereign Pontiff, who knew and esteemed him profoundly, to mountaineering in the Alps, and indeed, hardly a month after an Alpine expedition, during which he must have drunk some tainted water, he died of typhoid, not quite thirty years ago; and I mention even this that you may see how far removed is holiness from softness. . . . When he went to Berlin he had made a vow of chastity, which he preserved inviolate. Prayer and his daily Communion were the very foundation of his life. And what I want to emphasise in the case of this reserved, laborious man—so correct with his trimmed beard and city dress, so conscientious on committees—is the undeviating, utterly self-obliterating dedication of himself to God *within* his profession. Ozanam's unbelievable devotion to the poor expressed itself, as it were, parallel with his career; Ferrini offers the perfect example of a man who *within* an absolutely unimpeachable public and professorial life, maintained a vision of extreme sublimity, and offered, with extreme intensity, every beat of his heart, every outreaching of his soul, to God through Jesus Christ. He died October 17, 1902.

Would that I could relate something about Dr. Necchi, also of Pavia. Born in 1876, he became a doctor, married most happily, became adored during the Great War, first as doctor in a mountain artillery battery, then in a field ambulance, then in a military hospital. Thenceforward he devoted himself increasingly to the study of all that we call ' shell-shock,' and of the methods that we group roughly under the title ' psycho-analysis.' His own interior life had not been placid. He knew by intimate experience the torments that an infinitely sensitive nervous system, imagination and mind, can undergo. Hence, together with his profound learning and manifold experience of men, came his almost miraculous healing power.

Impossible to describe the part Necchi took in all forms of social Catholic action; he should be the patron of all who wish actively to serve Our Lord. Enough to mention that it was he, under God, who brought to the Faith that companion of his youth, Gemelli, a leader of Reds, editor of a revolutionary sheet, then brilliant but agnostic doctor; then convert, friar, and first rector of the University of Milan, of which, one may say with respect, the prime founders were Gemelli himself, Necchi, and Pope Pius XI, when still Cardinal Ratti. Necchi, Franciscan tertiary, diagnosed his own mortal illness, and died serene, nay joking, like Sir Thomas More, after a day's work among his sick, just over two years ago. A hero, if ever there was one.

Forgive me if I rapidly mention here no more a professor, but a university student, Pier Giorgio Frassati, who died at twenty-four in Turin, July 4, 1925, and to whose funeral, as to Don Bosco's, the whole great city went. Why? He had seemed strong as a horse; almost too good-looking; dense black hair; tremendous mountaineer; a very jovial friend; much photographed—mostly in plus-fours and a pipe; training to be a mining engineer; determined to marry soon and have an enormous family. . . . What was there in that to put a population on its knees? To make a very anticlerical newspaper say that even those who could not share his faith were filled with 'reverent stupefaction' . . .? I could quote the entire page. His life, in Italian, which ran through five editions in a year, is being translated into English.

Enough, maybe, to say that every morning he received Christ in Holy Communion, and that in no hour was he separated from Him. He kept his magnificent young body in complete control; he consecrated literally every spare moment to the service of the poor; he died, after a lightning-swift illness, radiant and serene and totally unselfish. Aloysius Gonzaga, the young renaissance prince of horrible ancestry, described himself as a 'piece of twisted iron.' I can hardly see, in Frassati, even the beginnings of a twist. But he, like Aloysius, was *iron*. Over my bed I have a fragment of Pier Giorgio's writing, scrawled in anguish as he died. All I can

---

*Ludovico Necchi; by Mgr. Olgiati; excellently translated by H. L. Hughes; an admirable pamphlet. C.T.S.

ask is, that 'my last end be like his,' and that our young
university men and women, in every land, may obtain his
intercession.*

I conclude with a simple name, but a dear one—Matt
Talbot, a Dublin working man. Born in 1856, a very
troublesome schoolboy, he was put to work at twelve as a
messenger-boy in a store which did business with Guinness's.
At thirteen he came home drunk—on stout. He was removed
to the Port and Docks Board, and came home drunk on
whisky. At seventeen he became a bricklayer, and would sell
his very boots and stockings for the drink. 'Most nights'
he came home much too drunk to pray, and for some years
lived without the Sacraments. At twenty-seven he found that
no one would stand him a drink—he had always drunk all his
own wages and could stand nothing back. . . . Bitten to the
quick by this humiliation, he took the pledge for three months
and suffered so intensely that he swore to his mother he would
break it the moment the three months were up; but he began
to attend daily Mass at five, and received Holy Communion.
He never broke that pledge; and with the drink went his habit
of cursing. From then on he chose to sleep on a couple of
boards, and to pray, and to fast. He became a workman in a
timber-yard; the cheeriest of companions, in fact, rather
rough in some ways, he ended by dominating by sheer *character*
his environment; he never rebuked; he never started 'religious
talk.' Yet theft ceased; obscenity ceased; he refused to lie.
During the dreadful Labour troubles and Larkinism of 1913–14
he sympathised whole-heartedly with the cruel injustice dealt
to his fellow-labourers, yet refused to join in manifestos or in
picketing, and renounced strike-pay on the strength of it. Yet
such was the perception among his fellows that he was on a
different plane, that they refused to refuse him their assist-
ance . . . but the money went in helping men poorer still
than he. In the troubles that ensued, and during the Anglo-

*E voi altri italiani, a cui giugne in Italia l'omaggio reso della mia patria
lontana a questa gloriosa figura di Piemontese, di Italiano, di Cattolico
. . . e chissa che non sia in un domani non lontano . . . a questo
Beato!

Irish war, and during the Great War, he refused absolutely to take part in any political discussion.

This man, who went to bed at ten-thirty, rose at two to pray; at four he dressed and went, about six, to Mass; at eight, to work. During the day he might take a cup or two of cocoa and a couple of potatoes; hardly ever meat. He worked, with increasing responsibility, extremely hard; during any interval he prayed. When his mother (with whom, in their great poverty, he shared a tenement-room) died, his prayer became, you might say, continuous. His spiritual notes survive. He could not spell; but he could talk to God. His chief reading was the Bible—especially, of course, the Gospels. His friends were innumerable; his charity, immeasurable. You find a formula: 'The men loved him—Matt had no use for money.'

In 1923 he felt ill; he went to hospital with a bad heart; in 1925 he died in a Dublin street.

He had written: 'The Kingdom of Heaven was promised not to the sensible or the educated, but to such as have the spirit of little children.' May this broadcast have echoed something, at least, of his folly. 'Stronger than men,' said St. Paul, 'is God's weakness, wiser than their wisdom is God's folly.' Had the world's politicians and financiers the spirit of Matt Talbot, they would achieve that peace and union between nations and races that at present is nowhere to be found.

AFTERWORD
and
SUMMING UP

AFTERWORD

I venture to remind readers of this small book that the pages inserted between the 'talks' about the Saints were not spoken through the microphone, and that the B.B.C. is in no way responsible for them. Not that I see anything objectionable in them, though they may contain some historical opinions with which not everyone would agree. But, then, almost every historical opinion, and perhaps every philosophical opinion, is disagreed with by somebody; and no one is at all likely to agree with all that has been broadcast from Savoy Hill or from the new home into which the Corporation emigrated. (I wish it luck. The inscription in its vestibule is a noble one, dedicating as it does the whole work of the B.B.C. to God, and praying that no evil word, but only what is good, may reach the listeners' ears.)

In the final 'talk' I shall have to try to sum up what I have been saying, and to extract the Saints' specific qualities, so to say. I have nowhere disguised the fact—indeed, it has been publicly commented on—that I am a 'Roman Catholic,' that is, a member of the Church which owns as its supreme authority, and as Christ's uniquely constituted and guaranteed representative upon earth, the Pope. Yet in the concrete I do not find, and correspondents do not seem to have found, that this interfered with my saying what I wanted to or demanded that I should vituperate, or even mention, anyone whose religion is not mine. No vituperation of myself, I may mention, seemed to come from well-informed or even educated sources. Nor does that surprise me, for I wanted merely to relate the history of certain men, the purity, nobility, and enduring value of whose character and work no one, I imagine, would wish to dispute.

But I have, in sincerity, to add that I do not find their true equivalent among any other set of men, even Christian, and certainly not pagan. Whenever you read a biography you do much more than obtain a knowledge of mere facts. You pick up a 'taste,' an aroma, an impression of the man in question; if you do not, the biography is no good. If you read Plato's biography in Latin, with all the proper names left out, you still ought to be able to say: 'This man was a Greek.' No one could mistake a book by a Theosophist for a book by a Catholic, even though no one formula could be taken exception to. The whole flavour of the thing would be different. Hence, I hold that anyone who seriously studies the Lives of the Saints (not at all like William James, in his *Varieties of Religious Experiences*, for example, of whom you could forthwith say with certainty that he never from the outset had the faintest chance of understanding what he was talking of), is bound to detect a difference in *quality* between men who believed as these Saints believed, and those who did not. People may or may not like their special 'quality,' and may assign quite different sorts of origin, educational, psychological and so forth to it; but there it *is*.

Their sort of holiness is a quite special thing; and I cannot deny that it seems to me to have been produced within, and fostered by, the Catholic environment, creed, and practice, and nowhere else. God knows there is virtue, very high virtue, virtue that any man may envy, elsewhere too; but, I repeat, Saints are Saints because they were *holy*, and holiness is rare—so rare that many may never have had the chance of observing it. They can observe it in the Lives of the Catholic Saints, if they read them with the Catholic mind, but apart from that mind they will hardly interpret them with any complete success.

*

SUMMING UP

This is the fifteenth Sunday on which we shall have been talking about Saints. I ought to try to make some sort of a summing up. I thought, at first, that the very word 'Saint' might make the talks distasteful. I was wrong. Letters from men and women of very many different 'denominations' have proved this.

The chief regret expressed has been that nothing was said of women-saints. Perhaps the B.B.C. will double its courtesy by allowing me to speak of them later on.

The other chief reproach was that I spoke of men who lived 'so long ago.' Still, before I was half finished I got a postcard saying that 'the Saints have got us moderns beat every time.' But that was *because* I had only half finished. I purposely chose examples of sanctity from various lands, from different classes of society or different occupations, and from every great period of history, *up to our own*, to show that Sanctity was not an affair of century, nationality, or caste. You have had a German, Italians, an Egyptian, an African, Frenchmen, an Englishman, an Irishman, Spaniards; and you could have had names from Australia or Canada. You have had a king, men of imperial descent or of mercantile parentage, university men, peasants, a very humble working-man, soldiers, lawyers, doctors, priests, and laymen.

Now, what have I really meant by 'Saint'? On the whole, in these talks I have related the exterior part of certain lives. I do not think I have neglected their innermost life-springs; but I have wanted to be concrete, to give dates, to put in colour, to make the man (so far as I could, in a quarter of an hour) solid and alive. Now we must try to get underneath all that, and seek for just those life-springs.

Yet first I want to say that I have meant to speak about something that is very *great*. Something quite different from what the life of 'worthies,' as they say, or remarkable men (let

119

alone 'unusual' persons), or prominent or even pious personalities could possibly be. I have been talking of something
that outpasses normal humanity infinitely further than
Faraday or Kelvin outpass a little boy in his elementary
school; or than Livingstone or Stanley outpass, as explorers,
lads who have hardly left their village. Does that mean that
the Saints have been non-human? Freaks? Monstrosities?
Not in the very least. If Hermann, Xavier, Don Bosco,
Matt Talbot, have seemed to you inhuman, I have failed
indeed. Once and for all, the Catholic believes that the Son
of God took up into Himself Humanity and all that is in it;
and the Saints retain all the human nature that is in them,
all their personal temperamental, hereditary, educational
characteristics, just as they had a nose of one shape and not
another. They retain their tendency to gentleness, or to
imperiosity; to sense of humour, or to sense of sublimity
(or to both); to timidity, or to audacity, as much as anyone
else does; if they are vividly intelligent men, they do not
become dolts; if they are very simple men, they do not turn
into philosophers.

What, then, have these Saints that is 'special'? They
believe in, act upon, and bank upon *with total conviction,*
things that most of us believe in *vaguely.* They do not think
that this world is an illusion or a dream, for it is not. But
they know that it is perfectly meaningless apart from God
who is its Creator and who created it for a purpose, and each
of us within it for a purpose, and so, that we create chaos, if
not crime, *apart from God.* Could we have lived without
father or mother? Could we breathe without air? Could
we hope, if we knew we were coming to nothing, or, that
there was nothing to come to? No. For the Saint, God is
our Origin ; God our Environment ; and God our End.
But that is not all. In some sense or another, the Brahmin,
the Mohammedan Sufi have known that. *The Saint has
been a Christian.*

I repeat (and I speak now not as a Catholic, but just as
one who loves to study history and the lives and minds of
men who have lived, or who live), the Christian Saint is

unique in human records. He is quite, quite different from the Buddhist, from the Persian Zoroastrian, from the clients of Occultism or Higher Thought, or what not, and by a whole world different from the humanitarian or the philanthropist or the earnest Uplifter. Quite, quite different. No one who studies facts can go astray about this. He may object to the difference, but he cannot deny it. All the good stuff that the Buddhist or the Uplifter possesses is in the Saint, but there is also something else that is quite different.

The difference is first and foremost this: the Saint lives at an elevation, with an intensity, with a perseverance that are not, and that he knows are not, due to himself. All the catch-words: Self-suggestion, Sublimation, let alone Altruism or In-Tune-with-the-Infinite-ism, or what not, sink into absurdity, and, indeed, a horrible vulgarity, once Saints are being talked of.

The Saints are, as St. Paul says, ' In Christ,' and in them ' Christ lives.'

In these talks I have said little of the preternatural experiences or powers of the Saints. I have not said much, so far as length of sentences goes, of their union with God by prayer, of the penances by which they detached themselves from any sort of worship of earthly idols, or of the ' miracles ' they worked—that is, the kind of thing they did which might be expected from a man who relied in no way on his own powers, but whose work was ' on the scale of the energy of the right of *His* strength ' who ' energised so mightily ' in *them*. The Saint was a man who essentially did not do an unthinkable amount of human work by means of human will-power merely. Men who do, either are helped, oh, by quite human means, such as tobacco, alcohol, strychnine, nervous tension, success, applause; or need holidays, experience reactions. They try to hold themselves up by means of their own ideal, as a man might try to hoist himself into mid-air by the hair of his own head. . . . Saints are *men* who are *super-natural*. Super-naturalised. Their actions, bodily or mental, thus constantly rise higher than their human source because of that added thing that is to be called Grace—

God's ' free gift '—which is *so* added, however, as to be
infused throughout their Self, so that they are not merely
pulled about by God's power, like marionettes, but act wholly
as men, yet super-naturalised men; and their ' activity ' will
never have to be measured by weight or bulk or number,
still less by mere exterior or material results. What they
do in virtue of their union with God, our Lord, may be quite
invisible, yet eternally significant.

Hence you will not wonder if the Saint seeks almost instinc-
tively to be *like* Christ; and also tends to disentangle himself
from everything he possibly can that might interfere with
that likeness and that perfect union. No question whatsoever, in a Saint, of working for his own career, or name, or
wealth, or comfort. Lest he be deluding himself, he will try
rather for total effacement, personal humiliation, poverty as
complete as possible, nay, suffering itself; for, though no
Christian morbidly worships Pain as such, he knows very
well that Christ's Life worked out into His Passion and His
appalling death, and he will become wretched if he sees his
own life issuing into ease, let alone luxury, or frivolities, or
mere wealth, or notoriety. And, in short, it isn't argument,
but *direct love* for Christ, that makes the Saint want to suffer
for, and along with Christ; and, indeed, he will do so, deepest
of all, within his mind and heart, and enter with Christ into
His agony, because having that ' mind ' which was ' also in
Christ Jesus,' his heart will break at the sight of the world's
great sin: its injustice, cruelty, lust, and pride—all the forms
in which Self-worship can express itself.

Hence the penances of the Saints; hence their mysterious
interior crucifixions. There is herein nothing of the self-
torturing fakir, any more than there is fanaticism in their
zeal for other men; not the least trace of gloom in their
renunciations, of self-righteousness in their condemnation
of this limited world when it sets itself up as ' good enough ';
or of prudery, timorousness, scrupulosity in their very flights
from what might too strongly tempt them. Their whole life
becomes an adventure, an enterprise. Who can suppose that
Camillus, Vincent de Paul, Peter Claver, failed to perceive

the bodily pains that human nature suffers from and did a super-heroic work to relieve them ? But poor, nay, downright paganised, had been their vision, had they not perceived within all that, causing all that, alone putting the gall and the vinegar into that, the only ultimate evil, Sin, which rots souls and imperils their eternity.

The Saints, then, saw all that bodily exterior pain, nay, even the mental sickness that is the consequence of false ideas within the mind, *as a symptom* of something far deeper, because spiritual; and, when they anointed the leper, bandaged the ulcer, their eye and their love reached the soul, its sorrows and its sins.

And the race of Saints never dies out. Why should I fear to say that I have met lives of true heroism, that may, indeed, have implied a destiny of Sainthood ? Not for me, assuredly, to say that such or such an one *is* a Saint, or even is destined to become one. That is for God to judge of and to make known, and for divinely-sanctioned authority to announce, in the case of those men and women whom He may wish to proclaim and placard before human eyes. But, remember, it is not the proclamation nor the placarding that *makes* the Saint; God makes him.

Saints, then, are not men of one period, place, or temperament; not morose or kill-joys; not fanatics or obscurantists; nor inexplicable portents among men. They start at the beginning—God; God revealed in Christ. They move towards man's only End—God; God reached through Christ. Christ is their Light, and so they are not deluded; Christ, their Way, lest they should sit idle; Christ, their Bread, lest they should faint in their long journeying; Christ, their Life, even now, so that in Him they become Good Shepherds for the world; and Christ their Life hereafter, so that in Him they live, and in Him are energising still amongst ourselves.

May God give Saints to our country and our times; may Christ dawn again so vividly for us that the germ of sanctity which exists in every man may come to what it *can*, and our lives be enriched, inflamed, intensified, purified, Christianised, Christianising, uplifted and lifting others till we become

' sons of God ' through Him Who for our sake took flesh and dwelt amongst us, Jesus Christ, Himself the Son of God and Son of Mary, the crown and queen of Saints.

' Give me souls,' prays the Saint. ' Give us Saints,' should pray our confused, tormented world.